Praise f(

CW00664393

The Silent Fem

"Rosjke is a strong voice in the struggle for mothers and women to be heard, valued, and nurtured. So turn up the volume and listen closely, you're about to make some powerful changes. This is the missing life manual for mothers and daughters alike."
Dawn Berry, Burstintolife.com

"We need more books like this and more women prepared to stick their heads above the parapets."
Stephanie Hale, Oxford Literary Consultancy

"This world needs more voices like Rosjke's that empower mothers to be strong and courageous for their daughters and sons, creating a new legacy of respect and love, not only for their families, but also for the community (or society) at large."
Tina Coombs, Vice-President, Women's Federation for World Peace International

"Rosjke's writing is so eloquent and life changing."
Estelle Read, Beee, Training and Coaching

"*The Silent Female Scream* describes an emotional freedom and empowerment that is so essential for women's visibility, rights, and voices to be heard loud and clear."
Anne Perry, Director, Power Service Derby

"*The Silent Female Scream* is a must read for counsellors and therapists who work with women and men."
Ivis Kennington, Counsellor & Psychotherapist

"Rosjke outlines a refreshing new look at why women are taught to suffer from low self-esteem."
Claire Kirtland, Star Communities

The Silent Female Scream

*"Learn how to believe that as a woman
you have the right to be heard, valued and respected,
and to know that anything less is just not okay."*

Rosjke Hasseldine

Published by Women's Bookshelf Publishing 2007

© Rosjke Hasseldine 2007

Rosjke Hasseldine has asserted her right under the Copyright, Designs and Patents Act 1988 to be identified as the author of this work.

All rights reserved. No part of this book may be reproduced or transmitted in any form or by any means, electronic or mechanical, including photocopying, recording, or by any information storage and retrieval system, without permission in writing from the publisher.

First published in Great Britain in 2007 by:
Women's Bookshelf Publishing Ltd.
www.thesilentfemalescream.com

Many of the stories that appear in this book are composites; individual names and identifying characteristics have been changed. Nevertheless, they reflect authentic situations in the lives of the many women the author has seen in her practice over the years. If you think you recognise yourself in these pages, the similarities are strictly coincidental. The author's own stories represent her experiences and memories exclusively.

Please note that the author of this book does not dispense medical advice or prescribe the use of any technique as a form of treatment for physical, emotional, or medical problems without the advice of a physician, either directly or indirectly. The intent of the author is only to offer information of a general nature to help readers in their quests for emotional and spiritual wellbeing. In the event you use any of the information in this book for yourself, which is your constitutional right, the author and the publisher assume no responsibility for your actions or the outcome.

ISBN 978-0-9557104-0-7

United States Copyright Office Registration number: TX 6-889-000

Artist: Ele Pack
Author Photo: Michael Lau, toadimages.co.uk
Cover Designer and Typesetter: Commercial Campaigns
Printed, bound and distributed by Lightning Source UK

Permissions

Anderson, J. (2000). *A Year by the Sea: Thoughts of an Unfinished Woman.* (New York: Broadway Books). Reprinted by permission from Random House, Inc.

Baber, K. M. and Allen, K. R. (1992). *Women & Families: Feminist Reconstructions.* (New York: The Guilford Press). Reprinted with permission from The Guilford Press.

Bassoff, E. S. (1992). *Mothering Ourselves: Help and Healing for Adult Daughters.* (New York: Plume). Reprinted with permission from Penguin Group (USA) Inc.

Braun Levine, S. (2005). *Inventing the Rest of Our Lives: Women in Second Adulthood.* (London: Viking). Reprinted with permission from Penguin Group (USA) Inc.

Reprinted by permission of the publisher from *MEETING AT THE CROSSROADS: WOMEN'S PSYCHOLOGY AND GIRLS' DEVELOPMENT* by Lyn Mikel Brown and Carol Gilligan, pp. 73 and 80, Cambridge, Mass.: Harvard University Press, Copyright © 1992 by the President and Fellows of Harvard College.

Buchanan, A. J. (2003). *Mother Shock: Loving Every (Other) Minute of It.* (New York: Seal). Reprinted with permission from Avalon Publishing Group.

Kindlon, D. and Thompson, M. (2000). *Raising Cain: Protecting the Emotional Life of Boys.* (New York: Ballantine). Reprinted with permission from Random House, Inc.

Northrup, C. (1994). *Women's Bodies, Women's Wisdom: Creating Physical and Emotional Health and Healing.* (New York: Bantam). Reprinted with permission from Random House, Inc.

Northrup, C. (2001). *The Wisdom of Menopause: The Complete Guide to Creating Physical and Emotional Health and Healing.* (London: Piatkus). Bantam Books 2006, (revised edition). Reprinted with permission Christiane Northrup, M.D.

Northrup, C. (2005). *Mother-Daughter Wisdom: Creating a Legacy of Physical and Emotional Health.* (London: Piatkus). Bantam Books, 2005. Reprinted with permission Christiane Northrup, M.D.

"Saplings in the Storm," from REVIVING OPHELIA by Mary Pipher, Ph.D., copyright © 1994 by Mary Pipher, Ph.D. Used by permission of G.P. Putnam's Sons, a division of Penguin Group (USA) Inc.

"Men in Relationships," from THE COURAGE TO RAISE GOOD MEN by Olga Silverstein and Beth Rashbaum, copyright © 1994 by Olga Silverstein and Beth Rashbaum. Used by permission of Viking Penguin, a division of Penguin Group (USA) Inc.

Excerpts from ODD GIRL OUT: HIDDEN CULTURE OF AGGRESSION IN GIRLS, copyright © 2002 by Rachel Simmons, reprinted by permission of Harcourt, Inc.

Smith, B. (1995). *Mothers & Sons*. (Sydney: Allen & Unwin). Reprinted with permission from Allen & Unwin Pty Ltd. www.allenandunwin.com.au

From *The Beauty Myth* by Naomi Wolf, published by Chatto & Windus. Reprinted by permission of The Random House Group Ltd.

Wolf, N. (1993). *Fire with Fire: The New Female Power and How It will Change the 21st Century*. (New York: Random House). Reprinted with permission from Random House, Inc.

From *Misconceptions* by Naomi Wolf, published by Chatto & Windus. Reprinted by permission of The Random House Group Ltd.

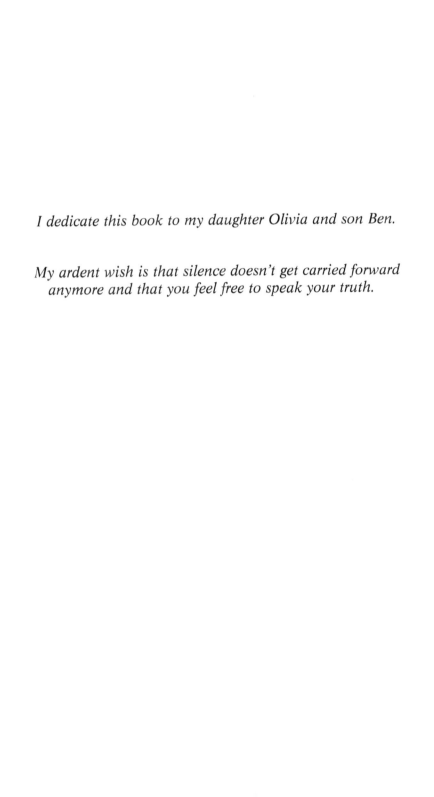

I dedicate this book to my daughter Olivia and son Ben.

My ardent wish is that silence doesn't get carried forward anymore and that you feel free to speak your truth.

Contents

Part Three: Being Myself in My Relationships

Introduction

*We can all recall moments when we didn't follow our
inner voice. When fear that we wouldn't be liked,
or someone else's thoughts or needs, or our inner insecurity
about whether we were allowed to feel or want
screamed so loud in our heads, we got drowned out.
What we knew to be true, or what we needed to do or say,
or our anger or hurt got pushed aside as we followed
what others expected us to do, say, and be. – RH*

Betty Friedan wrote about women's silent scream in 1962, calling it "the problem with no name," in *The Feminine Mystique*. Forty-five years on, women are still screaming and it still doesn't have a name. Even though women's lives have changed dramatically since our grandmother's day, I am not sure our emotional lives have changed all that much. We have certainly won the right to vote, to have a career, to control our fertility, and we enjoy far many more freedoms than our grandmothers and mothers ever dreamed possible. Yet emotionally, females are not in good shape. Too many girls are suffering from low self-esteem and anxiety, and are starving themselves to be acceptable. They are tearing at themselves and each other because they don't know how to say what they really feel. Women too are constantly worried about looking fat, feeding the diet industry with their hard-earned money rather than themselves, and suffering from low self-esteem and uncertainty as to whether they are allowed to say "no" or tell the truth about what they feel and need. Too many girls and women have not learned what it feels like to have a life that is centred on what is right, nurturing, caring, and doing the best for ourselves. We don't know how this thinks, feels, or behaves like, and epidemic numbers question whether this is even allowed or possible for girls, mothers, daughters and women.

Mothers are exhausted. They are losing themselves in the caring for everyone else and not themselves. Families and motherhood are way out of balance when the mother is viewed as, and is expected to be, the main carer, without any recognition for her nurturing needs. Mothers today, not unlike our mothers and grandmothers, are suffering in silence as the uncared-for carers in the family and world. Also, the emotional landscape between husbands and wives has not shifted too much since our mother's day. Too many wives are still feeling unloved, unappreciated and uncared for, and feeling the unequal burden of emotionally feeding their relationship with their husband or partner.

During my many years of working as a psychotherapist specialising in women and mothers and daughters, I have heard story after story of girls and women silencing their screams. I hear how they struggle to be heard and have their feelings and needs, especially their emotional needs, valued within their relationships. There are too many of them for it not to be reflecting a theme. These courageous girls and women have helped me discover what it feels like to be female in a world that can only be described as still very much afraid of females speaking out, demanding and being angry: A world that is afraid of really hearing how females are being treated and knowing that the silence around a mother's emotional needs damages her relationship with her daughter and her daughter's relationship with herself. These women have taught me how the rules of silence and the experience of screaming without being heard harms our relationship with ourselves, and how each experience chips away at our spirit until we learn to silence ourselves. They tell a story that warns against being complacent about our progress as women. It warns that underneath the equal opportunity legislation lies a different emotional reality that hasn't moved very far from our grandmother's day.

These wonderful girls and women have helped me realise that the problem with no name has always had a name. It is *women's silent emotional needs*. That is why I have called this book *The Silent Female Scream*; it illustrates the collective female legacy and experience of being silenced. Our grandmothers and mothers grew up during times where women's silence and invisibility was especially acute. Many daughters today, and I am one of them, grew up with mothers who did not have a language for, or who did not feel entitled to speak their emotional needs. These mothers could not teach their daughters how to speak their emotional needs.

Forty-five years on from *The Feminine Mystique* and having had the first and second wave of feminism that won us legal rights and a growing entitlement to have a voice, we are in desperate need for a new revolution, a revolution that teaches us how to feel entitled and equal within ourselves. If females are to ever enjoy complete visibility and equality, our emotional reality has to reflect that. It has to catch up and believe that *"every female has the right to be heard, valued and respected, and to know that anything less is just not okay."* This is *The Silent Female Scream Revolution's* motto.

In this book, I will teach you how to live by this motto, how to claim your voices and feel entitled to speak and be heard, and what to do when, and it will happen, this "new normal" is not welcomed by others. I will teach you how to create a life that nurtures you, feeds you, and empowers you to create a new normal in which your needs, rights, truth, and boundaries are as real as you are. The questions I will ask you and the stories I will tell of my clients' journeys and my own journey will help you on your way. They will help you create lives in which women flourish, feel emotionally fed, feel strong and entitled, without entertaining any flicker of doubt or uncertainty as to whether you are allowed to, or even should be asking anything for yourselves.

The Silent Female Scream Revolution is a wake-up call for girls and women everywhere to dare to speak—to start speaking with a voice that expects to be heard, whether it is convenient or not, whether others want to hear you or not. Whether or not there is a pervasive fear that your voice will change the dynamics and roles within the family and rearrange the responsibility for nurturing. This world needs women's voices—whole, truthful, emotionally honest and vocal.

The journey will take you through three stages that are reflected in the book's three parts. In Part One we learn about how females are still being silenced. We need to be awakened to how silence behaves, and to how it punishes through subtle and powerful messages of guilt and fear for not fitting into the "nice woman-good girl" mould. In Part Two, we learn to understand how we have internalised the messages that silence, and how they have disconnected us from our voices and ourselves: how the messages we received from the women and men in our life have taught us to silence ourselves and doubt our entitlement to speak. I invite you to take this most essential life-giving, life-changing and future-changing journey that will decontaminate you from your learned silence and claim your voices. The questions I ask at the end of each chapter are like nurturing food that will feed the emotional hunger that is created by silence.

In Part Three, I focus on claiming your voices and being yourselves in your relationships with the women and men in your life. I will look at the mother-daughter relationship and the father-daughter relationship, amongst others. Women's emotional silence requires that we look at our relationships with both the male and female influences. Fathers are extremely powerful. The mother-daughter relationship cannot be understood without examining the father's attitude toward women speaking out. It helps us understand our mothers better, and the patterns of silence we might have continued with our partner or husband. Understanding the culture of emotional silence within the male culture is essential for our relationship with our sons as well. Mothers have huge power in teaching their sons to either continue the emotional silencing of women and men—which we will look at in depth in the mother-son chapter—or not.

Silence damages all our relationships, especially our relationship with our daughters and sons. Having gone inward first, you are now ready to have your new way of relating to yourself reflected in all your relationships. You will learn how to stop feeding from only crumbs of attention, because you will no longer see your worth being reflected in being silenced, being treated as less equal, and being invisible. Slowly, voice by voice, moment by moment, your world will start to change. And then, because of the changes you have made for yourself, the whole world changes.

By taking this journey you aren't just changing your own life, you are changing the lives of the women and men who will come after you. This is why I am calling it a revolution: claiming your own visibility and equality is a political statement. It will change the world, one woman at a time, one son at a time, and change the lives of your daughters, granddaughters, sons and grandsons. For a mother to learn to connect with herself is the most powerful, healing, and change-making journey she can do for her daughter, because it is only through hearing herself that a mother can hear her daughter and pass on the conversation that teaches her daughter how to hear herself. It will also challenge the damaging power of emotional silence within the male culture and teach her son to remain emotionally intact and able to hear and respond to women's emotions.

I believe that a mother claiming her emotional needs is key to healing women and the world. What I mean by this statement is that when we open our eyes to our own mother's emotional needs that were never recognised, it heals us, heals our relationship with our mum, and creates the conversation that will help us on our journey of mothering ourselves. Mothering is a core part of what women do, which isn't exclusively meant to mean mothering our own children. It means mothering ourselves, empowering ourselves to be the person we want to be and learning to recognise and meet our own emotional needs.

This is my revolutionary wake-up call for women. It reflects the wake-up call I needed and had, which is reflected in the stories I tell about my own journey, and that my clients needed and had. It is a wonderful moment when you suddenly wake up to knowing something you have somehow learned to not know.

If you are reading this book, you are already on your journey of becoming awake yourself. I invite you to see yourself reflected in the stories I tell in this book, whether it is a story of one of the many brave women profiled here, or my own. Women learn the most through hearing what other women have been through and how they have survived. The details might be different; we might live in different cultures and countries and speak different languages, but the themes of silence are often the same. I must warn you though; the journey to being fully awake isn't easy. The voices of others and a society that is afraid of women knowing their minds and speaking their voices will not be happy. They will turn up their volume in protest. The more we speak and know and reclaim ourselves, the louder they will protest. But don't be discouraged. The journey is worth it. Worth it, because as a client once said to me, "My feelings are precious." She had suddenly become wide-awake to herself after having been asleep to her feelings for most of her life. I thought her words were beautiful. They said to me that she had become awake to how her learned anxiety about speaking about herself had hidden a great truth: that her feelings, needs, and voice are precious because they speak about who she is.

This revolution calls for an equality that isn't about being equal through being like men. It encourages girls and women to discover their individual and collective female ways of doing and being. It claims our right to have our way valued as being just as valid and just as important, and our mothering ability, our relational way of being, all our voices respected without question.

Remember that no woman is an island. We need to ask for support, for encouragement, for feeding during this difficult journey. Keep away from people who discourage, who question, even if they say they have your best interest at heart. They do not! Surround yourself with good people. With women who encourage, who are also learning to speak, and who will not need you to compromise being able to speak for being loved.

Go well on your journey to claiming your liberty and voice.

With all my love,
Rosjke Hasseldine

Part One: Being Silenced

1: What is The Silent Female Scream?

Women's voices have been silenced for generations.
We have been taught to fit around what others think,
others need, and to feel wrong when we speak our truth
with passion. This kind of wounding has left its scars
on every mother and daughter. – RH

The idea for this book came to me about fourteen years ago while I was sitting in the impressive Indiana University basketball stadium watching my first college basketball match. As I watched the athletic young men passing the ball around the court at breakneck speed and the female cheerleaders jumping and cheering from the sidelines, it struck me that I was watching more than just a basketball game. I was watching the interaction of women's and men's place, power, and visibility in action. In the young men, the heroes of the game, I saw how men are still the ones making the goals, making history, and having their achievements celebrated and reported in the newspaper, whilst, like the cheerleaders, women still look on and cheer from the sidelines.

As I watched the cheerleaders, I noticed they all looked as if they had been cast from the same mould—prepubescent bodies, blonde-to-light brown hair, thin, young, athletic, short-to-medium height, wearing the same short skirt-and-top set. It was as if they were selected not only on their athletic ability, but also on how closely they reflected the image of a sexually attractive female of today. Their similarity in looks was too much of a coincidence for it not to have been intentionally crafted.

Watching them made my stomach queasy. Though their athletic ability was impressive, I couldn't ignore what I was seeing reflected in their position and purpose on the court. To me they looked devoid of uniqueness and individual identity. They looked hollow, as if their bodies, their looks were all that was required, wanted and valued, a shell that required hours of preening and a level of thinness that undoubtedly meant enduring the daily pain of dieting and believing that denying themselves sustenance would get them noticed and valued. But what was even more difficult to watch was how they had somehow accepted that their visibility *did* depend on their looks, and on how well they entertained without grabbing all the limelight for themselves. I wondered how it felt deep down, when in the next day's newspapers and in the trophy stand, they would be forgotten in the glory of the male team's goals, games conquered, and titles secured.

What disturbed me was that these young women were expected to not mind that they are forgotten . . . not mind they are packaged goods who had to be grateful for being selected as a cheerleader. And they certainly did look as if they didn't mind. They seemed oblivious to the fact that they could expect more: that they could expect to be the ones on the court making the goals, winning the games, and being cheered and clapped. In their made-up, cheering, hollow bodies, they looked as if they had swallowed their limited value and identity in total, without question. They had learned to believe it was an honour to be cheering on the male team, that the only way of being visible and having value was through their connection to a powerful history-making, goal-making, game-winning man. And in order to secure this powerful goal-making man, they had to look right, act right, and endlessly cheer him on.

So where were the female basketball players? They were there, but without the fanfare, resources, or status. Tickets to the Indiana University basketball games played by the all-male team were expensive and hard to get hold of. The University was very much behind this team, crowing with pride about its reputation and success. The Indiana University women's basketball team's presence was harder to recognise. Tickets to their matches were easy to get; they were given away free at the local bank. And when they played, the event went by largely unnoticed, judging by the lack of traffic that streamed toward the stadium with their red-and-white scarves and flags flapping from the cars as they lined up, inching forward in eager anticipation of that afternoon's game. Their success was also unnoticed on the front pages of the next day's newspaper.

I didn't go to any more matches after that first game. Not only because the tickets were too expensive, but also because I couldn't bear to watch how these young girls had learned to silence their scream to such a degree that they seemed, outwardly anyway, completely accepting of their invisibility. But as the days and years have passed since that game, my discomfort hasn't gone away. In my clients' stories and in my own life I see the same invisibility, the same silenced expectations. I see the Silent Female Scream.

What is the Silent Female Scream? We hear a silent female scream anywhere where females have silenced themselves out of fear. Fear of not being heard, of being criticised or ridiculed. Fear of invoking anger or disagreement they fear they cannot stand up against, fear of loss of rights, promotion, services, livelihood, or even life. The Silent Female Scream is present anytime a female is trying to speak her truth but isn't heard, and then learns to believe that her words don't matter anyhow. The Silent Female Scream is present when a female's needs and feelings are not respected and instead are turned around as if it is her failing or her fault.

Being silenced is crazy-making. I have heard so many stories of women being silenced because they have spoken too strongly, too directly, too honestly, which somehow has the effect of giving the listener the excuse to completely ignore what they have said. These women are silenced by either being ignored, or through criticism and defensive remarks that turn their feelings around to be their fault or a symptom of something being wrong with them. Criticisms like being selfish or demanding: "How dare you?" or "How dare you upset me?" or, "Well, we all know that you don't get on with your mother." Over time, this can turn a sane-speaking female into a crazy-screaming madwoman because she isn't being heard.

We start off speaking normally, but as we experience being ignored or criticised over and over again, we become a little desperate. We start thinking of ways to get heard. We speak again, perhaps louder or with different words, in the hope of being heard. We keep trying, with more volume and more effort, screaming to be heard, but each time we are ignored or rejected until we become this crazy-screaming madwoman. Still we keep trying, because we hope that the next time it will be different or that *they* will change. Of course, in a culture where angry females are bad females, crazy-screaming gives the listener a perfect excuse to ignore us and label us as "an angry bitch," "abusive," "out of control," or "out of her mind." And that is what it actually feels like. It feels bad, wrong, crazy, and out-of-control. But if we haven't learned to recognise the language and belief system that silences us, we have no defence against feeling bad. We don't know that *it is the way we are being silenced that is wrong*, not us and not our words.

The pain of being silenced is excruciating. It can be too much to sit with, which leaves many females making the choice to turn their invisibility inward, against themselves, and blaming themselves for not being heard. They learn to think, "It doesn't matter anyway"; "It is understandable they didn't hear me, I'm this screaming, angry woman"; or "She has a lot on her plate, she doesn't need me to add to her burden." And over time, if they say it enough times to themselves, they will eventually learn to believe it.

But the good news is, our silence doesn't go away. Whenever anyone or a topic is silenced, not recognised, treated as if they don't matter or the topic isn't important, a void is created. In this void is our Silent Female Scream, silent but still very real and present, because silence doesn't necessarily mean that the words, feelings, or dreams don't exist. They are just voiceless. If we take the time and listen very closely we can hear that, in this silent void, a woman needs to speak, a woman needs to cry out, and a woman needs to speak her mind. She may be physically present, but without her voice, she is invisible.

And what I have found is that even though our words may be silenced, our feelings always find a way to speak. They speak through the symptoms of depression, anxiety, eating disorders, or any other form of self-harm. They speak through our lack of self-worth or our invisibility in our relationships. They speak when we have learned to put others before ourselves: when a young female values her relationship with her boyfriend more than her relationship with herself, and when a mother feels guilty when she takes time for herself. They speak when we believe that we have to plead, beg, be really nice or be manipulative in the hope of being heard. And they speak when, inside, we wonder if it is our fault that others get angry when we speak or ignore our needs and feelings, rather than placing the responsibility on those who do not treat us with respect.

How many females have experienced someone asking them, "What do you need?" Not many. By the blank stares I get from my clients when I ask them this question, I know that too many females are never asked this question. This question creates anxiety, because we aren't used to answering it. Why not? It is a simple enough question. But in a society that is afraid of females becoming too vocal, too strong, too able to claim their power, it is a dangerous question. It knocks against a deep and unacknowledged fear of women exposing the uncomfortable story of how they are treated, or the fear that, if allowed, women might take over or they might stop taking care of everyone.

The truth is that silence damages everyone, males and females. It damages our sense of equality and rights. It damages the balance of power and our visibility. It stops us from recognising how damaging it is when we see mostly men leading countries, mostly men being asked their opinions, and see adverts that tell us we are flawed and need to buy this product or that lotion in order to lose weight or look younger. It discounts the wounding that silence inflicts on our relationship with ourselves while our truth and knowing of ourselves is chipped away, voice by voice, as we learn to believe that speaking the voices we are *told* to speak is normal and acceptable. But it isn't normal or acceptable. As we will discover, being silenced is more than wounding, it is dangerous.

2: Our Silenced Voices

*The definition of a "good girl" hasn't
changed much since our grandmother's day.
It still means fitting in, fitting around,
giving in to what others want us to do, and
definitely not upsetting anyone. – RH*

One particular day, I could literally feel my voice crumple away inside of me, like a piece of paper that is scrunched up into a ball before being tossed into the bin. I noticed this scrunching-up as I lowered my head, as if by lowering my head I activated the off-switch that turned off my feelings until they no longer existed and I no longer felt them. And in the silence where I used to know myself, I could only hear, in that moment, my supervisor's voice as I took on her truth, her words and her feelings as my own.

All this happened in a split second during my monthly supervision session with a woman who had been my supervisor for over four years. She was my advisor with whom I processed my psychotherapy work. Yet something interrupted my connection with myself during that particular session. I am certain that this disconnection had happened many times before without me being aware of it. But this time, I knew what was happening. I knew that I had somehow crumpled myself away and discarded my voice. I don't understand what was different on that occasion, or why I so suddenly became aware of how I silence myself. But whatever it was, I am grateful it happened. I needed to become awake to how easily I crumpled away my feelings until they seemed to no longer exist.

The issue that facilitated my awakening was a rather critical problem for any therapist. A client who was seeing me during her rather nasty divorce had started making serious threats to shoot her soon-to-be ex-husband. She said that she was at the end of her rope and had had enough. She was tired of having her contribution to the marriage constantly belittled and unrecognised. She felt voiceless against her husband's rejection of her existence and a legal system that treated her protests as the proverbial ravings of a woman scorned. She felt powerless against her husband's decision to walk out the door and set up home with someone else. And she was angry that he had left her alone to care for their three young children without showing any sign of being willing to play his equal part. In her pain and desperation, she had started to fantasise that shooting him would make it all stop.

I decided I needed to talk to my supervisor about this client's threats. I rang her up and asked her if she had a little time to talk with me about a rather critical issue. She responded in a cold voice, saying, "Why are you ringing me?"

At first her question shocked me, because I thought the answer to that question was rather obvious. It was my responsibility to ring her and talk through sticky issues like these. It was also her responsibility and role as my supervisor to guide and support me. I hesitated to answer her, because I didn't know how to respond. I felt a flicker of anger flip about in my stomach, but it didn't have the strength or conviction to be voiced. So, I did what I had learned to do long ago when I sensed my voice wasn't welcome: I ended the conversation quickly.

As I put the phone down and heard the click of the call being disconnected, I felt my anger at her unwillingness to respond to my need to talk evaporate. In its place, I felt that familiar feeling that I had done something wrong by calling her, that I had demanded too much, was making a problem out of nothing, and had disturbed her when I shouldn't have. I felt that I should have been more competent at sorting this problem out for myself without having to bother her.

In the days that followed, I debated between telling my supervisor how I felt about our conversation and just leaving it. One part of me knew I needed to speak, that speaking was my way of honouring my feelings and claiming my needs. Yet another, more powerful part of me was afraid: terrified that speaking would make her angry with me, or criticise me for wasting her time and not being competent enough to sort this issue out myself, which in either case would leave me feeling wrong again. I wanted to avoid feeling wrong for not doing what she wanted, and to evade feeling bad for asserting my needs. But that would have meant ignoring her obvious discomfort in tackling this issue with me.

In the end, I decided to speak. I knew my fear was only alerting me of my long-held dread of being "not good enough" rather than some real, life-threatening danger. I realised that my fear needed to be kindly acknowledged, and then challenged and healed as Susan Jeffers suggests in her book: *Feel the Fear and Do It Anyway*.

During our next meeting, I tentatively started to explain what I was feeling. But after I had spoken only a few sentences, my supervisor leaned forward and interrupted me, saying, "Oh no, you have misunderstood. I was only asking you what do you want from me."

Again I felt that knowing flicker in my stomach as I silently said to myself: *I thought what I needed was plainly obvious, so why did you feel you needed to ask me?*

But no sooner had the flicker taken shape than a much stronger feeling extinguished it. It was that all-too-familiar feeling I had wanted to avoid: *I am wrong again because I asked and said too much*. It was then I noticed that as I lowered my head, my feelings and needs crumpled away and vanished as I quickly picked up another client's file and changed the subject.

Later that evening, feeling confused and unsure about what had happened with my supervisor, I rang a friend to ask her what she thought. As I explained to her the situation, she became outraged. At first I was taken aback by her reaction. Then, her anger started to thaw my silence. It was wonderfully reviving to hear her anger about how I had been made to feel wrong and responsible, when I had done the right thing from the beginning, as any ethical therapist would do. Her anger gave me strength, revived my nearly extinguished self-knowing, and exposed how much of my "good girl" and "nice woman" training had invaded my sense of rights without me knowing it.

I didn't realise how much I had learned to believe that "good" and "nice" women do not demand, and do not keep expecting and asking when they intuitively sense that their feelings and needs aren't welcome. These women believe that nice women think of others first. They respond to what others want and need above their own needs and wants. And if their own needs and someone else's needs are in conflict, they willingly forego their own in favour of the other person's. I was being a good girl who grins and bears the silence around her feelings and needs, since a good girl doesn't complain, doesn't ask for something for herself, even if what she needs is essential.

This was the first time I knowingly felt my feelings crumple away, the first time I became aware of how I disconnect myself into no longer existing and how I turn into a "good woman" who is oh-so-quiet, compliant, kindly, and sensitive to everyone else's needs. I had become a good but silent woman who had lost her healthy protective voice and sense of responsibility for herself. I had, in effect, silenced myself because I didn't know any other way of behaving. From childhood, I was taught to silence myself by being surrounded by women and men who silenced women.

As I thought about my client's struggle to be heard and my own, it shocked me to realise how similar we really were. Both of us were fighting against being silenced. My client was murderously reacting to her husband treating her as a non-person. She had to fight because she couldn't allow his treatment to become her truth. I was fighting to keep my needs alive and not allow my supervisor's resistance to my needs and fears about my client's situation become my truth. We had both been silenced, and we both were learning to speak and keep hold of our truth against forces that were uncomfortable with our truth and needs.

As I reflected on how easily and unconsciously I disconnected and silenced my voice, memories of prior silencings started to bubble to the surface. I remembered sitting in a meeting with two men, four women and the head of the student placement office at Indiana University. It was the beginning of the academic year, and we were employed to supervise student teachers while they were on placement in local schools. This was our first meeting of the year and my first year in the job. I was excited and apprehensive about meeting my colleagues and starting this new job.

After we had all taken our turn to introduce ourselves to the group, the leader assigned us a team-building task. The exercise was to build a shelter out of newspaper and tape with only ten minutes to discuss how the six of us were going to build a shelter big enough to cover all of us and then ten minutes to build it in complete silence. As I remembered participating in the exercise, I was shocked to notice how compliant I was during the planning. I hadn't realised how emotionally and intellectually absent I was then. I don't remember at what point I disconnected from myself, but I silently complied with what the two men thought was the "best" way of building the shelter. I noticed I wasn't the only one silent. Most of the other women just went along with the assumption that the two men were in charge of the project and the two men just assumed that they were in charge, each vying with the other for the position of absolute leader. I remembered how I nodded in agreement and smiled while I accepted the job one of the men assigned me. But one of the women didn't take too easily to the men's commands. She spoke up and put forward her suggestions, but somehow her voice and energy got pushed aside. I remember feeling uncomfortable with the tension in the group around her assertiveness, and feeling she was being awkward and difficult, that her speaking up was working against the group's task.

Looking back, I now see that this woman wasn't being difficult. She was more alive and real than I was, and didn't "put up and shut up" like I did. She still knew her voice, her thoughts and her needs, and she wasn't dead silent like I had become. It is frightening to recognise how easily I had learned to believe that for me, a woman, being silent, silenced, treated as unequal and invisible, was normal. How did I, my client, our mothers and grandmothers, all of us, learn to disconnect from ourselves and travel far away from the baby girls we once were, who screamed loudly whenever we needed something? How did we learn to organise our needs and feelings into boxes that labelled some as acceptable and others as not acceptable? Where did we learn that other people's needs, feelings and rights are far more important than our own? And how did we learn that being good and nice means being silent and compliant?

3: Taught to Be Silent

I had learned to become a female impersonator. I learned to switch myself off before I even realised I had disappeared from my own radar. And in the silent no-knowing, I learned to mould myself around what others want and around being "nice" and "kind," taking care to never cause upset or make anyone angry with me.

I like Mary Pipher's definition of a female impersonator in *Reviving Ophelia.*[1] Girls become "female impersonators" who fit their whole selves into small, crowded spaces. Vibrant, confident girls become shy, doubting young women. Girls stop thinking (or are never taught to ask themselves), "Who am I?" "What do I want?" and start thinking, "What must I do to please others?"

She warns how becoming a silenced female impersonator means being in danger of becoming a selfless puppet: a woman who has little or maybe no conversation that asks herself, "What do *I* need? What nurtures me and fits in with what is respectful and nurturing of my life?"

How did I become such a female impersonator? How did I lose myself so easily? Where did I learn to believe that when a woman speaks up or resists others from taking over or taking charge without her express permission, I viewed her as being difficult, demanding and not "nice"?

As I ponder on these questions, I hear a number of voices rolling about in my head. I hear my client Jill's hurt voice, telling me that she was accused of being "insular" after she said no for the first time in her life. I hear Lauren[2], a teenage girl, speak about how she has learned that honesty isn't appreciated in females. I hear my mother-in-law pass on her lessons of female compliance to my teenage daughter. And I hear my father say that girls are demanding and more difficult to bring up than boys.

All these voices tell a story of how women are taught to be silent, socialised to adhere to the code of acceptable female behaviour that moulds our sense of who we are, or more accurately, who we are expected to be—a code that tells us in many direct and indirect ways that anger, unavailability and selfishness, which is all code for thinking about our needs, are ugly things for a woman to show. A code that makes us uncertain about ourselves and afraid of our healthy will power, and far too keen, in a frightened sort of way, to fit into being "nice."

I will start with Jill's story. After over half a lifetime of being supportive, helpful and oh-so-available, she finally said no to a request from a family member. It was true that she didn't have the time to help at that moment. But truer was her growing tiredness of always saying yes and ignoring her own feelings and needs. She was starting to wake up and realise that everyone just expected her to help, and her efforts to fit her life around others were never acknowledged or thanked. Though she felt good about having said no for the first time and for putting herself first, her pride in herself was short-lived when everyone in her family "tut-tutted" at her with angry looks and voices, warning her that she was becoming "insular." She hadn't expected this reaction and it hurt her deeply. She had hoped to get warm words of encouragement and praise for making a stand. She didn't expect to be criticised and told they didn't appreciate her new, tentative attempts at focusing on herself.

As we talked about her experience, she realised that her family wanted her to be the all-available one. Her sudden effort to take control over her time and become more self-focused was threatening the balance of care and nurturing in the family. She had long felt unsupported and invisible in her family, and now she knew why. She was invisible outside of her "helper" role. She had been taught from childhood to see herself as a helper, and no one had voiced any thoughts or questions that she could expect, or choose, anything different. She had learned her lessons well, and it was scary to suddenly include herself in the list of people who needed to be recognised and cared for. It meant stepping away from her helper role and learning to stop defining her worth around being needed.

Jill cried when she realised what she had feared for all those years had actually happened. People suddenly stopped liking her. They didn't like it when they could no longer call on her time. And because being needed was so entwined with her sense of worth, not being liked cut her deeply. It made her feel more alone than she could ever remember feeling.

But as she thought about it, she also wondered if she had been feeling this alone for a long time, but hadn't noticed in her flurry to be oh-so-helpful. If perhaps her keenness to help others had, all along, masked her deep loneliness because she didn't like feeling it or acknowledging it. It was too raw a truth that, in her family, acceptance and love were conditional on complying with the code of helpfulness.

I encouraged her to explore her painful understanding of herself and her invisibility in her family. I explained that, when we grow up in a family that treats love as conditional, we have little choice but to mould ourselves around its conditions and become the acceptable female they want us to be. But eventually, the conditions become too painful to keep complying. Our spirits can no longer tolerate the restrictions, the lack of nurturing, and the disconnection from our true selves. This was happening to Jill. She had had enough. She was ready to understand the restrictions and conditions she had learned to accept, and to dare herself to relearn that true love is never conditional: to relearn that the only life for a woman *isn't* in selfless service to others, but that we are entitled to create a life that feeds and nurtures us. Finally, I helped her understand that her spirit was speaking through her pain, and like all of us, she needed to change in order to survive.

This brings me to Lauren, an adolescent girl interviewed for the study *The Harvard Project: Meeting at the Crossroads—Women's Psychology and Girls' Development,* conducted by Lyn Mikel Brown and Carol Gilligan.[3] Lauren stands out for me because of her clarity in speaking about the pressures and punishment girls suffer when they speak and behave outside of the female code. In the study, girls were interviewed at various ages as they progressed through adolescence to discover how girls disconnect from themselves and lose their voices.

At eleven, Lauren had already worked out that "by being herself and staying in genuine relationship, by not leaving in the face of conflict but saying what she feels and thinks, Lauren has reason to believe others will find her abrasive, obnoxious, insensitive to their needs. And people do seem happier when Lauren does not say what she feels."

Secretly, women know this to be true. I heard an entire class of university students admitting to knowing this to be true during a lecture on gender. We know that the price for getting "too big for our own good" or "too big for our boots" is social exclusion. We all hear the code that is imprinted in the many sayings that cut females down to a much smaller, more acceptable size.

It is hard to fight against such pressure and keep connected to our voices, beliefs, will power, rights, and anger at injustice. I have noticed that in England, females get cut down through having their words scrutinised. I have been accused of, and also heard other women being criticised for, using harsh or strongly descriptive words. As if somehow we are not allowed to mean what we are saying, that it cannot be the way we are describing it. Is this just an English way to justify discrediting and then dismissing what women say, or does this happen everywhere? I suspect it is worldwide.

I remember the agony I felt as I wrestled with my own anger and silence when it was my young adolescent daughter's turn to be taught the age-old lessons of female selflessness. Olivia and I were sitting in her grandparents', my parents-in-law, living room one afternoon. Olivia was sitting on a large wing-backed chair crying. I cannot remember what event had occurred that had upset her, but I do remember she was feeling that she had been treated unfairly over something. At eleven she was still in touch with her voice, and she was letting us know that her strong sense of justice and fairness had been hurt.

As I sat with her, wondering what to say to her, her grandmother cut through my pondering and said, "Stop crying, Olivia. You need to stop crying because it is making your granddad ill, and then I have to look after your granddad."

I looked over to my father-in-law. He looked perfectly well to me as he sat quietly, trying not to notice what was happening in the room. As her words sank in and I watched my daughter swallow her tears and silence the volume of her sobs, the hairs on my back started to bristle and a wave of anger rose from my stomach. My anger was of being upset about my daughter's silencing and my own pent-up anger at being silenced for years. I had to struggle to not muddy the waters with my own years of forced silence, whilst not allowing my daughter to be silenced by the voices of my own and my mother-in-law's entrenched female code: the code that teaches females to clean up our anger, to sugarcoat it, and above all, do not upset anyone even though they have upset you. As I fought my own internal battle, I knew that for now, I needed to collect myself and deal with this incident only.

I was furious at my mother-in-law for telling Olivia to keep quiet, for telling her that her feelings of injustice weren't important, or even more, were invalid, and that she was bad for expressing them. So bad, in fact, that she was making her grandfather ill, and then she would be responsible for causing her grandmother extra work. I was enraged that history was repeating itself: that it was now Olivia's turn to be told that "good girls" think of how their feelings affect others, and then silence them because expressing them might upset someone.

As I sat with my daughter, I struggled to find the words to express my anger. I wanted to say something to protect and support her. Eventually, I fumbled something that resembled that I had different rules, and I allowed Olivia to cry when she was feeling angry and hurt. As I finished speaking, my father-in-law suddenly woke up from his emotional absence and tried to diffuse the situation by changing the subject. I let him, and the incident was never mentioned again.

What I wanted and needed to say was that I was bloody angry with my mother-in-law for dumping on Olivia the inaccurate and guilt-ridden responsibility for her grandfather's health and her own issues of responsibility for her husband. My daughter needed to be heard. She did not deserve to have the female code of thinking of others only, or her grandmother's discomfort with strong emotions, passed on to her. But all this stayed silent within me. Yet even though I didn't say exactly what was burning to be said, I think I communicated my support to my daughter. A few hours later, she came up to me and thanked me for sticking up for her.

I remember my own father instructing me with a similar message. He would say in a voice that was heavily laced with frustrated conviction, "Girls are so much more difficult to bring up than boys." I remember the murmur of agreement amongst the family and friends that heard his unsubstantiated truth, the murmur that allowed this belief to weave itself into the fabric of my family's and my own belief systems—that my moods, my irritations and my demands were much more difficult and consequently, more unbecoming than those of my brothers. I don't ever remember anyone explaining to me why they agreed with Dad.

My guess is that if girls are encouraged to express what we feel and need, the balance of nurturing and caring will change within the family. We won't be socialised to become selfless listeners, helpers, and cheerleaders of others. We will demand to be cheered on as well. We will grow up to be self-expressing, thinking women who challenge and change any power imbalance and gender inequality that exists because we won't tolerate anything less!

I like Christiane Northrup's words on this subject in *Women's Bodies, Women's Wisdom.*[4] She says that believing that boys are inherently easier to raise than girls can actually be no more than a self-fulfilling prophecy.

> *It makes sense to me that girls would get moody around the age of twelve or so. They can see what's coming. If girls are socialised to be passive and self-sacrificing, their powerful spirits don't like it! (If someone was actively trying to do that to me, I'd be very tough to live with.) If a teenage girl is taken seriously and encouraged to follow her dreams and speak her mind, she will be no harder to raise than a boy. Young women need to be cherished, honoured, encouraged to speak, and praised for their gifts. Otherwise, the world won't benefit from these gifts [and their thoughts and ideas], and the cycle of oppression will continue.*

Girls grow up surrounded by a wall of "be nice"; "play nicely together"; "don't say that, it isn't nice," or risk being shunned for being "too big for your boots" or "being all that." As Naomi Wolf in *Fire with Fire* and Rachel Simmons in *Odd Girl Out* point out, females today are struggling with an enormous double standard. On the one side we have "girl power," which encourages girls to think big, want big, and be able to do anything. Yet while we are dreaming big, we should also follow the code and be "chaste, quiet, thin, and giving, denying the desire for sexual pleasure, voice, food and self interest," as Rachel Simmons warns.[5]

How can we possibly do both? How can we realise our dreams *and also* deny our voice, self-interest, and needs? We simply cannot. These actions or intents are completely inconsistent with each other.

So where does this impossible double standard leave us? It leaves us feeling confused and stuck, and with a raging internal battle. Should we speak or keep quiet? Should we follow our heart's desire or should we feel guilty and worry about inconveniencing others? Should we tell the truth as we see it, or keep quiet because we may upset people? Naomi Wolf talks about her internal battle with what she calls "the dragons of niceness" as she struggled to keep speaking, to keep rocking the boat and not take any criticism as personal or a slant against her femininity.[6]

In a similar way to what Naomi Wolf expresses, writing this book left me wrestling with my fear of upsetting people and making others, especially family members, angry because I was writing about an uncomfortable truth. It was hard to not listen to these fears and to resist the temptation to water down what my heart yearned to say, to accept that some people will get angry, and that my message will shake the status quo at its foundations and threaten some people—and so it should. I too needed the encouragement that Naomi Wolf yearned for. To be encouraged "to be a bad girl in the interest of serving my voice," I too wanted someone in a respected position to say, "It's okay to make people angry. Change causes friction, and that is good. Tell your truth and fuck 'em."[7]

Sadly, no such permission was forthcoming, and my only option was to give it to myself. Like Jill, whose spirit demanded she start saying no regardless of the criticism, I dared myself to speak anyway and create a new female code, a code that helped me form a Teflon skin against the forces of silence: an outer skin that allows the messages of silence to just slip off, because inside, I know that a life that doesn't nurture me and isn't lived with myself at the centre, fully owned and in the driver's seat, isn't a life that I can survive. Anything less sentences me, sentences all of us, to a half-life as a female impersonator.

4: No One is Taking Care of Mum

*Women's willingness to sacrifice themselves for the good
of their children is something that our society—from individuals
to institutions—relies upon. It is useful leverage in pressuring
women of all classes into giving in, in different ways,
to unequal deals, negotiated hesitantly from the place of
weakness that is one's concern for one's child.*
Naomi Wolf, *Misconceptions*[8]

It was lovely how everyone greeted my news that I was expecting my first baby with such warmth and heartfelt congratulations. Women clucked and cooed as they kindly enquired about my health, and some were keen to pass on their wisdom. In the beginning, their attention and concern *was* lovely. But as my pregnancy progressed and the birth became an obvious reality, suddenly the focus of their questions was on taking care of my baby. No one asked me how I was feeling about stopping work, or whether I was planning to return to work after my baby was born; everyone assumed I was going to give up work and look after my baby.

Secretly, I hated their questions about finishing work. I never knew what to say. I was teaching at the time, and because my baby was due early on in the academic year, I was able to finish the year with my class. But explaining that didn't seem to say anything. In truth, I felt as if I was disappearing behind my bump, as if I no longer existed outside of it, as if I had turned into a big round incubator.

How could I be angry when everyone was smiling at me and looking happy for me? How could I say that their lack of asking about *me, all of me,* the parts that weren't about my baby's health and my pregnancy, left me feeling I no longer mattered except as a mother? And even if I felt I had the words, the courage, and the inner sense of entitlement to exist fully and completely and say how I was truly feeling, I knew they wouldn't understand, that they would feel I was making a fuss about nothing, that it was my hormonal fluctuations speaking rather than my truth. Knowing this made it all doubly worse, doubly silent, doubly invisible, and doubly uncertain.

So I did the only thing I knew to do at the tender age of twenty-three. I listened to the unmistakable message that now, as a mother, my career as a teacher or anything else I might be dreaming of doing was indefinitely over or at least on hold.

What other choice did I have? I was young, confused, unsure of who I was, and well socialised to pick up on and follow what *others* wanted. I was good at showing, on the outside, what I thought everyone expected from me, a happy mother-to-be who, with a sigh of contentment, waved good-bye to her life as she launched herself into motherhood. This seemed my only option, following the well-worn path laid out for me by my mother, grandmother, and great-grandmother.

But on the inside, hidden away from view, I was a ball of confusion, uncertainty, anger and fear that erupted late one afternoon while I was heavily pregnant and sitting in the car outside my husband's work while I waited for him to finish for the day. I don't recall why I was picking John up from work, just that I had waited a long time for him to emerge. Suddenly, my unvoiced fears burst forth in great sobs and gulps that soon steamed up the windows of the car.

As I cried, I became aware of an overwhelming feeling of being trapped in a life that was about waiting for others to be ready and fitting around everyone else's routines and needs. With horror, I saw my future identity and purpose being taken over by motherhood, that I was turning into my mother and grandmother, who had disappeared from view as they moulded their lives around the lives of their children and husbands as selfless servants. It wasn't only a career I was waving good-bye to, it was my life in which I existed as my own person.

Fear gripped my throat so tight, I had difficulty swallowing. I gulped in air to quieten the feeling of suffocation. What would become of me, the person I was before I had children? What would become of the dream of being the kind of woman who was in charge of her life, one who didn't defer her decisions and choices to anyone? All around me were mothers whose entire identity had been consumed by motherhood, where having anything of your own that wasn't about meeting your family's needs was viewed as being selfish.

Was this going to be my fate? Was I the only woman who was angry and resisting this fate?

When John eventually emerged from his office building and hopped into the car, I was still crying. He assumed I was upset for having to wait so long for him, and apologised for being late. He explained that his line manager had held him up, and he felt he couldn't say that his wife was waiting for him outside in the car. In his own way, he was feeling trapped by his manager's demands. As I listened to the reasonableness of his explanation, I swallowed my sense of loss and suffocation, dried my tears, and drove home. After all, I was looking forward to having our baby, and I didn't want to be thought of as a bad, selfish and ungrateful mother.

It has taken many years to realise what I agreed to in the silence of that late afternoon: to recognise the emotional disconnection, career damage, sexism, inequality, invisibility, responsibility overload and toxic guilt I had agreed to without knowing or recognising it. It took me years to become aware that no one once asked John what sacrifices and adjustments to his workdays and career he was going to make now that he was a father. As a father, no one expected him to make any adjustments and changes to his career goals. Rather, it was assumed and expected that I was to make all the space, all the adjustment and sacrifice, without question or complaint.

It is still shocking to see how alone, unsupported and blind I was then. Seven years later, when John went on a ten-day trip to the United States to interview for doctoral programmes, no one in my family offered me any help. No one, though I had two small children and part-time university study. Imagine if it had been me, and not John, who had gone to interview for doctoral programmes. Firstly, there would have been much "tut-tutting" about what I was doing. And secondly, John wouldn't have been expected to cope on his own. He would've had all kinds of offers of help with the cooking and childcare. Unlike with me, his need for support and some timeout would have been recognised and facilitated.

Waking up to the situations we find ourselves in involves much grieving. Yet I *needed* to feel how let down I felt by those who had cheered on my silence and ignored my needs. I *needed* to feel furious that large pieces of myself had been cut away and discarded because they were no longer possible, or consistent with my family's view of motherhood. Grieving was important to my awakening; it reclaimed the feelings and parts of myself I had long forgotten or never got to discover before the silence closed them off.

Today, it feels good to be awake. It is good to no longer believe that my jealousy of John's freedom to go to work, feel engaged in his work, and have his career suffer little disruption by fatherhood was not a symptom of my deficiency as a wife and mother. I am also finally free to no longer beat myself up for having been bored, because I now know that it wasn't a sign that I was an ungrateful mother. Rather, I was intellectually bored because something hugely important was missing for me: I needed something else apart from being completely engaged in caring for my beloved children. And it was wonderful to discover that I had protested, complained and realised that something was very wrong, even though I didn't understand what. My feelings of jealousy and boredom had spoken for me. My sobbing in the car before my son was born had spoken my truth. Even though much of me had been numbed down and desensitised, my voice had not been completely erased.

As I have become more aware of the pervasive messages of "good" mothering that surrounds all mothers, and listening to what other mothers say and don't say, I know I am not alone, that I am not the only one who has been numbed, desensitised or confused, madly juggling everything and never questioning it because I was too tired to sit down and ask myself "Why am I doing all of this?" Too tired to stop and ask "What do I need?", because I had so little energy left, all I could do was cope and tread water as fast as I could to prevent myself from drowning.

I know now that I was just one of an epidemic of mothers who don't realise that if they are frantically treading water, they are already drowning. I was drowning in my listening to others. Drowning in my numbed feelings, my self-criticism and guilt, my desensitised expectation of what I wanted for myself, my self-denial, my self-sacrifice, my juggling and my nurturing of everyone else except me, and my silence around the conversation that should ask, "Who is taking care of Mum?"

Now, some twenty years later, I wonder what reaction my daughter will meet if she chooses to have a child. Certainly, she won't be expected to give up her job, but sacrifices will be expected. Will her partner be asked what sacrifices he will make? I hope so. With great credit to John (and the growing number of fathers who are sharing the parenting with their partners and spouses), Olivia can expect to share the parenting responsibility of her child. Hopefully, she will have learned the conversation that asks, "Who is taking care of me?" and she will recognise when she's in danger of drowning and start saving herself. And hopefully, together with her partner, and many other mothers and fathers, she will force employers and society to change the long-outmoded and female-damaging paradigm that undervalues mothering and expects mothers to stop existing as themselves, as they juggle being everything to everyone. I hope Olivia and others like her will also challenge and change the outmoded male-damaging paradigm that doesn't recognise a father's need to nurture his relationship with his child.

Our family has to listen. Workplaces have to take notice. Voice by voice, we can expose the hidden sexism that is lurking just below the surface in reactions like the one that happened toward President Clinton, his wife Hillary and their daughter Chelsea while I was living in America. Chelsea had fallen ill at school and asked to telephone her father. The school, apparently shocked that she considered bothering the President, suggested she telephone her mother. Chelsea reportedly responded with, "Oh no, my mother is far too busy."

Whether this story is true or not, the "anti-Hillary" media reports about this rather innocent incident says everything about the expectation that mothers, not fathers, are responsible for the children's needs. Ignored by the media was a daughter's need to be with her father, a father's right and responsibility to nurture his daughter, and the rather obvious: even though President Clinton may be the president for a time, he will always be Chelsea's father. The same happened in the United Kingdom, when Prime Minister Brown cut short his family holiday to deal with summer floods and a foot-and-mouth crisis. Though that might be an important reason to break his holiday, no one asked whether it was okay for a father to just end his time with his family. No one asked what his wife thought, or his children needed, or suggested that even though he is the Prime Minister, he is also a father.

We all can lend our voice here. As a lone voice, it is difficult to change a rigid work culture or introduce a new normal into an entrenched family system. Alone, you are too easily brushed aside and labelled as wrong. But together, we are much stronger. When we gather together and say, "No, this isn't okay or good enough" when mothers are demoted, or treated as selfish, or when a father's responsibility to nurture his family isn't recognised by his workplace, a new normal can be created.

5: Where is Our Female Story?

Secrets are harmful. When a girl or woman is pressured or silenced to not tell what has been done to her, it harms her feelings of justice and her sense of her rights, and it shifts the responsibility back to her, harming her knowing of her worth. Secrets harm families; they erode trust and communication. And secrets harm the cohesion and balance of power within communities. When women's stories of violence, rape, incest, emotional abuse, domestic violence, loss, and grief are not talked about, it has the effect of condoning the behaviour. It makes the woman's experience mean nothing, as if it is normal, acceptable, "part of a woman's lot" as my grandmother would say. I have heard many women talk about how harmful it was for them, as well as their visibility within the family, when they couldn't speak about their experiences or discover and understand that knowing feeling that something is wrong. It shakes our trust in our instinct when we cannot enquire when we know something is being hidden. I am talking about that feeling we get in our bones that something is not right.

I would like to share with you a fragment of my story as a way of telling the story of what happens when our feelings are silenced, when we are left in danger of having it eat away at our insides as it changes from being someone else's shame into our blame. Silencing our emotional lives creates a triple wounding— the incident itself, the silencing of the incident, and then the shame we come to feel about it, as if it was our fault. We are wounded when we feel we cannot speak: when we don't know the healing balm of being heard and reacted to with understanding and shared anger. We all need to be heard, and be reminded that it wasn't us who committed the crime.

Let me begin with myself. I am a daughter, a sister, a granddaughter, but emotionally, I am alone. Although my mother and sister are alive, I cannot ask them for help, advice or comfort. It is a very painful truth to admit to, that for most of my adult life I have experienced one long silence from both of them. Long ago, Mum withdrew into an angry silence that prevents her from enquiring about how I am or what I have been doing. Admittedly, it is the norm in my family that women don't get asked how they are. We are the ones who are expected to do all the asking, checking-in and supporting, without expecting the same in return. But that doesn't seem to explain how heavy with blame and anger my mum's silence feels. It doesn't explain why my sister has chosen to side with my mother and add fuel to the story that somehow I am to blame for being ostracised, rejected, and ignored because I have done something so terrible that it deserves this degree and length of punishment. On days when their silence feels too cold and biting and the hollow emptiness that surrounds me becomes too much to bear, my mind frantically searches for a crimethat I could own up to, in the hope of having my mother and sister restored to me. But my mind can never find such a crime because there is no crime to be found.

Yet I am being punished. I have broken two fundamental codes of acceptable female behaviour in my family. Codes so strict, that if broken, they carry the sentence of being cast out. My first crime, if you can call it that, is that I could not follow the prescribed path of women in my family. As a girl I tried to be "good," but as an adult I couldn't give up my life and completely devote my days to caring for my family. I had to be me first. I needed to study, to have a job and a career, and to follow my dreams. My spirit needs to have a sense of my own life that isn't just about being a wife, mother and daughter, the all-available carer of both my extended and immediate family. But in my female family, that is a crime. Specifically, it is a crime against the sanctity of motherhood and femininity, which carries the charge of being a bad, incomplete, selfish kind of woman. There is no conversation that gives room for the women in my family to be a mother, wife, and daughter with a job and career or a sense of themselves. Being a wife and mother is all that I am supposed to want.

My second crime is that I could not cope with the code of silence that hung around my family like a thick blanket that could smother the loudest of cries. I needed to ask questions and to speak my truth. For women in my family, saying what we feel and what we think has no words, language, or acceptance. We are to suffer in silence and to carry "our lot," as my grandmother would say, with silent dignity. It is seen as unwomanly to burden others with our tales of the violence we have suffered, the abuse we have experienced, the dreams we have had to let go of. This code was extreme. It even dictated that voicing that we are ill and need some time out to recover is not womanly or motherly behaviour. We have to carry on regardless, for others, and never complain or demand, silently hiding the big and small feelings we hold in our hearts whilst always being available to others.

So, after years of banging my head against this code that wouldn't budge or change, it's no wonder that I too have stopped trying to tell mother and sister who I am. I have let the silence close in behind me as I take some comfort from no longer feeling battered and rejected every time I tried to be heard. But silencing myself wasn't an easy option. In the place where I need my mother, my sister, and my grandmother (while she was alive) is a vacant, barren wasteland that stretches as far as the eye can see: a wasteland that in one way tells me that the rules have won.

I have had to comply with the code of silence and silence myself because it became too damaging to keep talking and having my feelings responded to with angry silence. It was too wounding to speak and to be responded to as if I hadn't spoken at all. It became too hurtful to feel their anger and blame, and to repeatedly subject myself to hearing my truth twisted around and used as evidence to feed the story that I was bad, or "off the rails," which is code for being dangerous to be around. It was too emotionally stressful and damaging to keep trying while not letting their behaviour seep in and affect my sense of worth. It was like re-wounding myself over and over again. I had to put a stop to it for my own sake. Through my work, I know there are many women who know what this feels like. That they too have tried to survive in families and places where the only way to scream their silence was by walking away or shutting the door behind them.

It is a terrible thing to feel that you aren't welcome, that you don't belong, when somewhere you know that you do, because after all, they are supposed to be "family." It is the most confusing feeling to resolve when you have no place in your female family, yet your heart keeps yearning to feel loved, accepted and enfolded into their protective care. For me, it feels like a stabbing pain in the left side of my chest combined with a sense of being set adrift without my female roots, without oars and a navigation map to guide me, or having a female network that is there to cushion me when I fall. Without it I feel isolated, vulnerable, never completely sure if people will really do what they say they will, never really certain if I am totally welcome, and always anxiously checking that I can take care of myself.

Yet when I step aside for a moment from my painful isolation and I look at my female legacy with more objectivity, I can recognise the threads that have led to my silencing. From the few stories I know about my Great-grandmother, Grandmother and Mother, and the wounding they have each experienced, I see how the code of silence and sacrifice is all part of that thread.

Clarissa Pinkola Estés reminds us in *Women Who Run with the Wolves*[9] that a "dead zone" can form around our ability to feel and respond to our emotions, when our pain of being hurt is silenced.

Without the healing balm of being heard, a dead zone forms, sealing off our ability to connect with our own feelings, which also means it seals off our ability to hear other people's feelings, especially those close to us. Dead zones make us essentially emotionally dead to ourselves and in danger of wounding others with our inability to hear pain.

Her words make sense to me. The women in my family did not get a healing space in which to feel heard. They were taught that their worth was dependent on how well they *accepted everything and took care of everyone*. This kind of silence created a dead zone that closed my grandmother and mother off, and blocked their ability to emotionally respond to themselves and also to others. A dead zone keeps away anyone who dares to speak the unspeakable, including and especially a daughter. It creates an unspeakable pain, a fear of speaking and no language to speak it with. Being alone with their pain, a dead zone is built as a cold, anaesthetising wall around the wound. It makes sense that the anaesthetised will have greater difficulty hearing and responding to other people's pain, especially if it is voiced by their own daughter.

In many families, silence has long roots. My story of silence starts with my great-grandmother. She was a missionary's wife in Dutch Colonial Indonesia, and when each of her children reached the age of six, they were sent back to Holland to be educated and to live with relatives for the rest of their childhood. This is spoken about matter-of-factly, as if it is normal to be parted from your young children for the sake of their education. I can only imagine the wounding this would have caused my great-grandmother and grandmother. Maybe my great-grandmother had to close herself off because the separation was too painful to anticipate and really feel. Her sacrifice for her children's education and husband's missionary work is never spoken about. Again, because it is expected of women to remain quiet and obey.

One of the few stories told about her gives me a glimpse of her anguish. It tells how she threw herself into her eldest daughter's grave as her coffin was being lowered. What speaks to me about this story is not what she did, but the tone in which it was told. It was not told in a soft voice to honour her pain and loss. Instead it was told in shameful tones, with an unspoken but clearly audible warning to anyone who lets their grief get out of control like that. When my great-grandmother's husband died, her daughter (my grandmother) stayed home with her because they didn't want her to "embarrass herself" again. Her grief was seen as shameful and shut away from sight.

This same story repeated when my father died. No one broke down. It was all very controlled and "acceptable." Why, I wondered, then and now, is showing pain and grief so great you no longer know what to do with yourself treated as something shameful in my family?

It is hard to know when my grandmother closed herself off. I guess it happened piece by piece, experience by experience, silent by silent loneliness. In moments perhaps like, when at six, she was sent to Holland without being told that she wasn't going with her parents.

Or perhaps as a teenager when she gave up singing, her most favourite thing, because the night before the performance, after months of rehearsal, the people in charge of her forbade her to perform her leading role. The adults in charge surely knew she was rehearsing for a performance, knew how important it was to her. But somehow, on the night before the performance, they told her she wasn't allowed to perform, because performing on the stage was unbecoming of a lady.

Or possibly her change came later still, when she was living in Colonial Indonesia as a wife of a chemist but with the same qualifications and credentials as her husband, yet her husband was treated as a hero while she quietly slipped into the background.

No, I could never ferret out when Grandmother closed herself off. I never heard her strength, courage and heroism celebrated, never heard regaling tales of how she brought all of her three children out alive after two years in a Japanese concentration camp during the Second World War. Nor how she hid medicines underneath the family's washing while the Japanese soldiers searched her home for the missing medicine. The stories of my grandfather's courage and my great-grandfather's philanthropy are all the stories told of the past.

Rather, I remember my grandmother as a silent, withdrawn woman, who could sit for endless hours at her dining table in her stifling-hot kitchen, oblivious to the conversation that went on around her. I will never know the secrets that lay hidden in her heart, or her painful memories that were never expressed. They have all died with her, and I feel as if I am left mourning the healing she deserved to receive and never got, grieving for the grandmother I never got to know and feel known by. Since my family rarely talks, I feel that I am the only one mourning, the only one who is noticing the loss, the voices never spoken, the information never passed on and the healing never received.

As a child I yearned to know her, to hear her stories, and to sit on her lap while we talked to each other. But the warning of my later rejection had already visited me. I had learned early that asking questions, "being demanding and nosy" as it was called, would upset Grandma, which then upset Mum. So like my grandmother, I learned to keep my questions close, unasked. I can only guess what enormous secrets of incest, abuse and infidelity lay hidden behind her silent withdrawal and emotional vacancy. I guess in her generation, leaving her husband was out of the question. I wonder if she lacked confidence in her ability to take care of her children, even though she was an educated and capable woman. Or was it because leaving would have felt too shameful, as if it was *her* failure for not being able to keep her marriage and the family together?

The truth about my grandfather's sexual abuse of one of his daughters came out after he died. When I found out, I felt relieved. It made sense because I had always suspected something was wrong. Too many clues were guarded too angrily for them not to be important. Secrets, no matter how well hidden, always leave clues for those who are searching. But as the truth came out, the conversation in my family quickly changed to blaming the victim. The unbelievable story being suggested was that

Grandfather used sex to control his daughter's out-of-control behaviour, painting him as the victim of his daughter, rather than his daughter being his victim. (I do not want to go into detail about this part of my family's history because some of the detail is not my story tell. For my healing and my claiming of my history, it is enough to write about how silence intended to protect an abuser damages everyone, and especially it damages the relationships in the family.)

I was dumbstruck while I heard this absolution of my grandfather, being told with such great conviction. I couldn't believe it at first, and literally wondered if my ears just weren't hearing properly. But as I protested against this story that sounded so ludicrous to me, I quickly realised I hadn't misheard, and that protesting was useless. The secret was being rewritten, and whoever challenged its recasting would be ignored or laughed off as crazy. It left me feeling as if my words were inaudible, because as soon as their sound left my throat, they were swallowed up by an infinite darkness that didn't allow anything to be seen or heard that didn't fit with the party line.

I knew I had to get away from this type of dark silence, because it has the power to make you feel crazy. Even now, I can feel the crazy-making confusion creep inside me. Did I dream all this? Am I making it all up? Through my work with women who hold family secrets, I know that keeping the secret, being the only one who seems to know, can make you feel a little crazy. It can leave you doubting yourself and wondering if you've lost your grip on reality—when the truth is the reverse; anyone invested in keeping a secret has lost his or her grip on reality.

But take heart. Not being able to keep a secret, however dark, is a sign of our spirit's health. Those of us who dare to speak are the healthy ones, even if we're the only one to speak out. Those who retain their spiritual health must *speak*, because without our voices we don't exist within ourselves. Without our words, we are in danger of creating a dead zone within our own hearts, which will not only disconnect us from ourselves, but from our daughters and others around us. This is why a true cleaning of "the feminine laundry" is needed. We need to ignore the threats of silence that instruct us to not wash the family's dirty laundry in public, or even in private. If we keep silent, we'll be agreeing that silence is okay and normal, and that women's stories don't need to be heard, healed or aired so they aren't repeated over and over again, in each generation. Unspoken, poisonous silence encases feelings and stories so they no longer have the language or permission to be spoken about. It points its crooked finger at the victim rather than the perpetrator, at the speaker rather than the perpetrator.

Keeping silent has disconnected the women in my family and closed us off from each other, as it does in all families that keep secrets. Occasionally, the family may get together, but emotionally they are disconnected. The key is to really know and truly feel that if you have been rejected for speaking, you are not the only one out in the cold, even though it may, at times, feel like it. Silence makes everyone alone. Dead zones block us off from sharing our collective knowing. It freezes the female wisdom that has been gathered from generations gone for generations now and to come. And it dries up the flow of this wisdom that needs to flow freely from mother to daughter, warning, warming and teaching each successive mother and daughter, generation after generation, about what women need, what women know, and what women are.

6: Why Do We Tolerate Being Silenced?

Where has the feminist movement gone? To where has the entitled fervour that fuelled our great-grandmothers to fight for women's political voice disappeared?

One of the first things I noticed when I moved to England in 1997 was that no one described themselves as a feminist. Feminism was treated as a dreaded "F-word." Friends and fellow therapists advised me not to mention that I use feminist counselling theory in my work; they said it could put women off. They warned it could label me as a "ball-crushing lesbian," as if being pro-women automatically makes you a lesbian and anti-male. When a friend read an early draft of this book, her first comment was, "It's rather feminist." Her tone shocked me far more than her words, since it communicated the unspoken advice, *Maybe you should tone down your message a little*. If my friend had been alone in her reaction, I could've brushed it off. But she wasn't. I have noticed young women react with a self-satisfied relaxation that believes the job of fighting for equal rights has been achieved, a reaction that clearly requires them to deny the statistics, news reports and women's own stories. Older women react with a fatalistic malaise, as though believing we've achieved all we are ever going to.

What has happened in the country that gave birth to the vision and ideas of Virginia Woolf and Mary Wollstonecraft? What has created this fearful resistance to speaking of things female, of speaking of feminism, of having the conversation that claims our right to create and ask for a better life for ourselves? What is arresting women's belief in equality? Is it a lack of understanding about what women have had to go through to fight for their right to vote, to speak in public, to go to work, to own and inherit property, to have legal entitlement to their own children, to choose whether to have a child (or not), and to be educated—all rights we now accept as normal? In part, I do think women are suffering from a general ignorance about how recently those rights were given to women. We have lost the voices of the past that told of what it was like for women: the struggles that sparked the first-wave feminism that demanded all women be granted the vote; the stories of the 1960s that ignited the second-wave feminism, which demanded greater equality and exposed how women have learned to accept discrimination as normal. And today, we are supposed to be enjoying the third-wave feminism, which seems to me to be too much about women fighting about what is the correct sort of feminism, rather than gathering together to fight for our individual and collective voice.

Yet underneath the call for rights and equality, the end to pay inequality and glass ceilings, lurks a greater problem that no wave of feminism has yet uncovered. I believe the fight for women's rights and voice has become derailed (and treated as unfeminine), due to an epidemic of low self-worth women are suffering from throughout the world. This might at first sound a little simplistic. But every woman needs to have some degree of self-belief and self-worth in order to claim her rights. Low self-worth, by its very definition, makes it harder to create a life that respects, nurtures, and sustains you. We have to believe in ourselves to start voicing our rights, and fight against the forces that don't agree, and we must feel a certain level of entitlement to say, "No, what I need is going to happen, whether you like it or not."

"Self-worth" and "self-esteem" are much-used but greatly undervalued and misused terms. As Naomi Wolf highlights in *Fire with Fire*:

> *Right now, women can't change the world until they can become comfortable with using power, and with understanding how powerful they already are. Self-esteem is not limited to feeling confident about oneself. The step past that is feeling confident about one's right and ability to change the world.*[10]

Self-esteem is an active belief that is more than just feeling okay. It feels entitled, powerful and in charge of oneself. It asks and demands with a certainty that nothing less than a life that nurtures us is acceptable or even sustainable. It is only this type of self-worth that has the power to change women's equality, visibility and place in our world. It holds the spark of entitlement and the belief that we can create something different for our daughters and ourselves.

Our right to vote started with just this kind of spark. We no longer question this right, but my grandmother was thirteen years old when women were given the vote in Holland. If she were born in the United Kingdom, she would've been twenty-two years of age when allowed to vote for the first time. But had my family been Samoan, my grandmother could never have voted; my mother and I would've enjoyed that right in 1990. When you put a personal face on our rights it puts it into perspective, and we see how recently the idea of women merely voting was an unthinkable abomination to many.

It took a groundswell of courageous women to challenge this long-held belief as they dared themselves and each other to think differently. They spoke out, became angry, and put their collective foot down, demanding nothing less than equal voting rights. This same fire needs to be rekindled for mothers' rights, gender-equal sports coverage, equal pay, equal numbers of women and men governing our corporations and countries, and valuing the power of being female and the mother-daughter relationship. Outwardly, many women appear to be in charge of their lives. They have jobs and careers and are financially independent. Yet, in women's thoughts, I don't hear the same level of independence that is reflected on the outside. Rather, I hear a learned blindness that no longer notices or questions when someone is demeaning or disrespectful or silences them.

I am talking about the kind of blindness that my client Joan was suffering when she told me that the chief executive of her company had recently addressed the gender balance in the management team by appointing a new female member. When I asked her what the actual gender ratio was on this team, she said one female and four men. I looked at her in amazement. Since when did "balance" mean one out of five? But as I looked into her dulled eyes, I saw that she had already been numbed to accept a gender balance of one woman to four men.

Another kind of blindness I heard in Kim's story, as she told me how she was allowing herself to be continually mistreated by her boss. Kim had a long history of being bullied and she was still experiencing it at work. Her female boss was ordering her about without any recognition for Kim's needs, what was reasonable, or what her actual role and hours of work were. She was also being openly hostile to her, treating her as if she wasn't a significant member of the team. Yet as she described what sounded to me like a soul-destroying relationship and workplace, Kim's words and voice sounded unsure about whether her feelings were right. She wondered whether she should just put up with it and try to keep her boss sweet. Kim's sense of entitlement had been damaged after years of being treated as someone else's punching bag. She needed to become sighted in order to save herself. Her blindness was leaving her in serious danger of having her self-worth damaged to such a degree that she believed that being bullied was normal, okay, and even deserved.

I know what it's like to find yourself going down that slippery road of having your self-worth and sense of entitlement eroded piece by piece, belief by belief, and feeling powerless to do something about it. That crazy-making twisting of reality where somewhere inside you, you know you're being mistreated and demeaned, but no one around you seems to notice that something is wrong. It can make you doubt yourself and wonder if you *are* crazy. That maybe, you're making it all up.

This happened to me during my first year as a university counsellor. Within months of starting the job, I realised that the contract I had signed was very different from the contracts the counsellors had worked under only a few years previously. As I began to investigate, it became clear that counsellors were being downgraded. This small, all-female department was slowly being reduced in power and status. As I asked around, trying to understand the department's history, I was repeatedly amazed by the apathy around this issue. Very few people talked about it. When it was discussed, it was spoken about with an attitude of fate that at times was tinged with fear. Fear for their jobs. Fear that if we challenged our contracts and upset "the powers above," they might think that having a counselling service wasn't worth the trouble and close us down. The more I asked, the more pressure I was put under to keep quiet and stop asking for fear of losing our jobs.

In any other situation, that would look like bullying. Until that time, I had never questioned authority figures. I had a history of being easily intimidated, but for some reason, this time I couldn't keep quiet. I was angry. I couldn't shut my eyes and just accept what I knew was wrong. I couldn't ignore that without discussion or resistance, a department, however small, can be so easily demoted in power just because someone wanted to do this. I also couldn't see myself working in an environment in which my colleagues and I were threatened into silence.

I cannot explain where I found the inner conviction and voice to question, to make a fuss, and to ask for reasons from people in powerful positions who didn't want me to ask, or to answer me. Nor can I explain why, this time, I wasn't afraid of being shouted down and made to feel guilty for upsetting everyone. There were times when the denied reality created the crazy-making self-doubt in my head, but somehow this time it didn't have the power to make me stop knowing what I was seeing. Also, my colleagues' anger that I was sticking my neck out and making our department more visible, which they believed could make our jobs less secure, couldn't stop me. It was extremely difficult to deal with, but it couldn't blind me to put up with what was not okay. Maybe this was my personal final straw of being silenced for too many years. Whatever the reason, I could no longer stomach being threatened into silence or having my value reduced.

Eventually my quest led me to an interview with the director of human resources and his deputy. As I sat with these two men in their interview room, along with my male union representative for support, the deputy director turned to me and said in a loud, angry voice: "You're wrong, you're just wrong."

As I looked at him and saw that he was incredibly angry, shaking his finger at me as if I was a naughty schoolgirl who needed a good telling off, I didn't crumple away or scurry for cover. Normally an outburst like this would shut me up for good. Normally it had the power of leaving me anxiously trying to make up for my bad behaviour, feeling guilty and worried that I had done something terribly wrong.

Not this time. I remember feeling coolly detached while I watched him spit out his anger. I knew that his anger meant that I wasn't wrong. I knew the only thing he had left to shut me up with was his anger. And I knew that he knew I was telling the truth, even though I'm sure at some level he wouldn't let himself know that. He was using the oldest trick in the book used on women: make her feel guilty for having said or done something wrong so she will go away, keep quiet, and let those in power do what they like.

Unfortunately though, in spite of my coolness and my clear head, that is exactly what happened. This meeting was the last said on the subject, because they just wouldn't acknowledge there was anything wrong. And in the days after the meeting, I realised I alone couldn't change a system or make these men see what they didn't want to see.

This experience was a significant marker on my journey to becoming sighted to how I allowed myself to be treated and how I have learned to treat myself. As a mother, I needed to become sighted to the toxic guilt I had learned to live with and accept as "a mother's lot." A guilt that made me juggle too much, question myself too much, and take on too much.

I remember seeing an audience on an *Oprah Show* completely agreeing with a mother who admitted she had never had a weekend away from her children, even though her husband had regular weekends away playing golf. I was shocked to see how desensitised these women were to the sexism and inequality they were agreeing to and accepting as completely normal for wives and mothers. The audience seemed to be accepting the myth that taking a weekend away for themselves would be too difficult for everyone and maybe neglectful of their children, whilst fathers were free to go away without being guilty of neglect because all the inconvenience was the mother's to bear.

This kind of blindness needs to be healed if anything is going to change for women. Let us dream for a moment. What if these mothers on *Oprah* had said, "I need a weekend away too"? What if they believed that they were entitled to weekends away or to share the care of their family, and believed that time for themselves wasn't neglectful of their children? That in fact, these things were necessary for them as women and mothers. What if they believed that their needs were an important part of the health of the family and not an inconvenience?

How different would that family, that world, behave and feel like for mothers and daughters! It would create a world in which mothers feel strong, whole, entitled, nurtured and full, mothers who are in touch with their needs and wants and aren't afraid to ask and expect them to be met. In workplaces, these mothers would no longer accept the discrimination they face when their commitment and reliability to their work is questioned when a mother asks for time off to go to her son's football match. They will react to the sexism when the father in the next desk is hailed as a good-old-new-age guy whose commitment and loyalty to his job isn't questioned when he asks for time off to go to his son's football match.

The good work being done through organisations that fight for equal pay and equal rights needs to continue, but they alone cannot create true equality. True visibility and equality begins with each individual woman believing in her own rights and building her own self-worth. It begins with each woman feeling entitled to make choices that respect her and create relationships that are nurturing of her. It begins with mothers learning to believe, without doubt or guilt, that in order to nurture and cheer on others they need to nurture themselves first. It starts with a mother teaching her daughter to have this level of confidence and power, so she doesn't unlearn her childhood dreams of being the "queen of the world" who rules, and is obeyed and respected.

Part 2: Speaking Out the Silence

7: Lessons in Hearing, Claiming and Speaking My Voices

*Girl power is not about how you look or act to impress.
True, lasting, solid, girl power is feeling completely entitled to
speak your mind, without a flicker of doubt or a pang of fear.
Until we have achieved this sense of inner entitlement, women
will never be equal, or free to speak their minds, as fellow
human beings. Without this kind of entitlement, women will
always speak with a fearful voice. – RH*

I use the following analogy with my clients to help them
understand how they have learned to disconnect from themselves
and their inner voices. I see women having a wonderful, glistening
pair of silver antennae sitting on top of their heads, a beautiful set
of invisible receivers that pick up on everything going on around
them, and importantly, within them. I know this may sound silly,
but it is true. Just think of what life would be like without them.
How else would we know what is going on? How else would we
know when someone is upset even though they haven't said
anything? When someone wants us to do something even though
they haven't asked? Or when our stomach churns into knots
because we don't want to do something, or be with someone, or
spend time on something, but somehow we think we should.

These wonderfully crafted antennae are extremely precious.
They help us connect with ourselves. They are our sage, our
wisdom, our guide to what we know, feel, need, and believe. They
act as a warning device that sounds out the alarm when we are in
any kind of danger. Without them, we would have no way of
knowing when something is right or wrong. They pick up on the

subtle truths that hang unspoken in the air, telling us when we can trust someone, or when they aren't telling us the whole story or are downright lying.

But our beautiful, precious, protective, all-knowing antennae have been hijacked, hijacked by fearful minds and beliefs that are afraid of women being in charge, speaking their minds and doing what feels right for them rather than what others think they should do. Our socialisation for caring compliance, the lack of conversation that asks what women need, and our "good girl" training have all hijacked our antennae. These factors have taught us to tune our antennae away from what we think and need to what others think and need. We can all recognise the moments when we picked up on what we know, or what we wanted, or what was right for us, but our signal wasn't strong enough. It didn't have the power to really hear and follow our knowing. Our voice was drowned out by a stronger signal, one that told us what others wanted. And with our training to be a "good girl" and our need to be liked well entrenched, we drowned out our knowing even further.

Having our antennae tuned away from our voices is extremely dangerous. It can lead us to make choices that aren't right for us, and in extreme cases, to not see the harm we are doing to ourselves. When we are tuned into the voices of others, our instinctive screams of protest get tuned out. We will no longer hear our internal warning system screaming to us that something isn't right or someone isn't right, or that we are following a path that won't make us happy.

Janice, now fifty, recognised that, at twenty-five, she didn't listen to her internal screams warning her against marrying her fiancé. On paper, he sounded wonderful. A good job, financially secure, pleasant, liked by everyone else, funny, good-looking. But emotionally, he didn't know how to respond to her. He didn't listen when she said what she needed, and he ignored her when she was upset. After twenty-five years of having screamed to be heard, she had come to the end of her proverbial rope. With the children having left home, she too packed her bags and started to build a life for herself.

As she talked of her regrets about not having listened to herself at twenty-five, I asked her how she could've known to listen to herself. Who encouraged her to turn up the volume of her internal screams? Who had asked her what this relationship felt like to her? Did he feel nurturing? Did he listen to her?

As she thought about it, she realised that no one had asked her those questions. She remembered saying something about her concerns to her mother, but her mother didn't listen. Both parents had told her that he was "a good catch" and she should be happy.

It's hard to listen to yourself when those around you don't encourage it, or even recognise how important your own knowing is. I went off to teachers' college ignoring my internal scream that I didn't particularly like teaching children. I went because my mother said I should. Her reasoning was that it was good training for motherhood, and a job I could do if I had to work after I had children. I was seventeen! I didn't want to be a mother! But I still went. I went because I knew doing so would give me eventual financial independence. I went even though my teachers warned me I was making the wrong choice.

Why? Why did I listen to my mother? Why didn't I listen to my teachers? Why didn't I recognise that my unhappiness during my first year was a big, flashing-red stop sign? Because at seventeen, my antennae had already been tuned into what others want. No one had ever asked me what I wanted. I didn't even know this question existed. And without this question, I didn't trust myself enough to know what I wanted. I was afraid to trust my instinct because I didn't understand it, and I was sure my family would see me as "selfish," "ungrateful" and generally "bad" if I followed it. I didn't know of any woman in my family who had ever said no and done what she wanted . . . and was loved for it. I know that Janice and I are far from alone. There is a silent, undiagnosed, and unrecognised epidemic of emotional disconnection amongst "nice" women and girls that is crying to be heard and healed. In this part, I welcome you as fellow travellers to reflect on your own experiences and messages that have silenced and disconnected you from your vitality, dreams, nurturing and inner wisdom. Give yourself the time you need to ponder on the questions at the end of each following chapter, and start retuning your ears to the whisperings you have forgotten existed. Listening to yourself will help you rediscover treasures you have forgotten you owned. And remember: the greatest antidote against female silence is speaking. Speaking, even though it feels scary and fearful and others don't like it. We've all been born with a voice, and it is our birthright to speak and be heard.

8: Claiming My Emotional Needs

Women are expected to be nurturing towards others and
to put their own needs aside. Because women
and care-giving are seen as synonymous in our society,
women who fail to live up to these expectations are
denigrated for not fulfilling their adult developmental tasks.
Kristine Baber & Katherine Allen,
Women & Families—Feminist Reconstructions[11]

It was my body that warned me I was deaf to my emotional needs. I was feeling exhausted and undergoing various blood tests to try to find out why. At one of these blood drawings, the nurse who prodded my arm to find my elusive vein said to me, "Of course you're exhausted, you're a woman. All women are exhausted these days."

Her comment jolted me awake. I knew she had just diagnosed my problem. I was suffering from female exhaustion. I was all given-out, exhausted, and hadn't learned to speak the conversation that honours my emotional and physical needs and replenishes the well from which I give. I had ignored the wake-up calls along the way, so my body had no choice but to turn up the volume to jolt me awake from my comatose state of abject self-neglect.

I was suffering from the crisis in female nurturing, a crisis that is a direct result of women's needs being dismissed and even actively suppressed for generations. Self-neglect has, for generations, been a female's badge of honour, and still today, females' needs are treated as shameful. Like most women, I had learned to trivialise my needs to hot scented baths, a walk, or a little time by myself to recharge my batteries. But if anyone asked me, "What do you need?" I would struggle to answer. I was in a long-learned pattern of giving myself away, putting others' needs ahead of my own, and even adopting other people's needs. I had been trying to survive in a needs vacuum.

But how would I have learned anything different? How would I have learned to speak my needs, when my mother and grandmother didn't speak that conversation? My female friends and their mothers also treated self-care as selfish. Where could I have learned to ask myself what I needed, when no one had ever asked me that question? All I knew was to copy the women who came before me and those around me, all who behaved as if asking what someone needed is something women do for others but never for themselves. I worried that my daughter Olivia had also learned this same lesson. I noticed how she sidled up to me one day and said, "I can see that you are busy, so don't worry about me."

Her mixed message made me stop what I was doing. As I looked at her, I saw in her body that she wanted something. But when I asked what she needed, she squirmed and wriggled in discomfort, unsure of what to say or whether she was allowed to say what was burning to be asked. My heart constricted as I saw her uncertainty and confusion, and I knew that the female curse of disowned needs, of being liked through thinking of others first, had already been passed on.

I knew I had work to do. I had to understand the long line of outwardly "needless" women my daughter and I had come from. It started with my grandma's gravestone, on which the following Dutch inscription is engraved: *"Lieve mamma die haar leven wegcyferde enalles voor haar groeiend gezin."* Translated, it reads: "Beloved mum who throughout her life selflessly gave everything away for her growing family."

The word *wegcyferde* describes someone who has relegated all personal desires and objectives to a particular cause, which for my grandmother was her family. Apparently, there is a lot of honour attached to the word *wegcyferde*. But as a woman and her granddaughter, I saw little honour in her selflessness. In fact, as evidenced by my own daughter's unwillingness to tell me what she needed that day, it had wounded us all: wounded our sense of entitlement and visibility, as well as our relationship with ourselves and emotional survival.

I am sure my grandmother didn't know that anything was wrong. She was a product of her upbringing and generation. She epitomised the selfless virtues of Virginia Woolf's "angel in the house." She didn't realise the damage she was expected to inflict on herself every time she discounted her needs and suppressed her feelings. She also didn't recognise the damage being inflicted on her each time she was ignored, squashed or shamed. Her words of advice to me on my wedding day gave me a rare glimpse into the depth of personal neglect she believed was normal for a wife, mother and woman. On a card, she had written:

> *Be spicy and willing!*
> *Be not fussy but thrifty!*
> *Nor bossy but lively!*
> *Be patient and tolerant!*
> *So you are sure of the love of your husband.*

My heart feels heavy with sadness when I remember her words. It is tragic how she had learned to believe that being loved is conditional on being good and compliant. What did *she* have to swallow, deny or tolerate to be sure of the love of her husband?

It also makes me sad to think about what she *didn't* write. She didn't write a thought of encouragement about how lucky my husband was to be marrying me. Or the needs I could expect to have as a wife and young woman. She didn't warn me never to sacrifice my relationship with myself for any role or person. She passed on all she knew without understanding it, questioning it, or knowing the wounding it held. She didn't recognise how much she had abdicated her responsibility for her own needs and how that left her daughter, my mother, responsible for her. She didn't see the connection between her burdened, stoic silence and how my mother spent her life in frantic worry about what her mother needed. I guess this means that she also didn't recognise how responsible she had felt for her own mother's needs and how wounding that had been to her. What I saw happening between my mother and grandmother had happened before, between my great-grandmother and grandmother. And if I didn't claim my needs, it was in danger of happening again, between my mother and I and my daughter and I.

The neglect had to end with me. Olivia's insecurity about asking what she needed was certainly a reflection of my own disowned needs. I knew she would learn to speak her needs with more confidence when I did. I knew she would learn to grow a deflective skin against the messages that shame female needs, when I had learned to grow my own. We both live in a society that has no conversation that acknowledges a woman's needs, and has an entire range of shaming labels and words designed to shut up any conversation that suggests women have needs that demand attention. Both Olivia and I have had too many experiences and witnessed too many needs being ignored, shamed, and stonewalled. We have had our needs turned around in order to make us look defective for needing. And we have been shouted down with anger or silence. We both know the words that are designed to silence and shame us into returning into our good-girl box: the accusations of being "selfish," "uncaring," "insular," "needy," "high maintenance," "demanding," and "greedy." And we also recognise the most seductive of silencing techniques, the "yes but..." The "yes but, what about so and so? Aren't you concerned about that?" They all retune our antennae away from ourselves by making us feel guilty.

Julie, a friend, telephoned me with a dilemma that reflects this crisis in female needs. She was feeling stressed and harassed about letting her daughter go to her father's (Julie's ex-husband) house on Sunday, even though Julie and her daughter and new husband were going away on holiday early the following Monday. She rattled off what her daughter, her ex-husband, and new husband wanted and needed, without mentioning herself. When I asked her what she needed, she fell silent. The question was completely foreign to her, and she didn't know how to answer it. Julie is like millions of women who have learned to be "yes" puppets who dance to everyone else's needs and expectations in a desperate attempt to make everyone happy. A "yes" puppet ignores that she is feeling stressed, harassed, tired and definitely not happy. A "yes" puppet has stopped seeing the emotional and physical cost to herself while she chops herself up into tiny pieces to fit in with everyone. She doesn't notice that the balance between her needs and other people's needs is way out of kilter until her body screams so loudly, she has to take notice.

As I have discovered, this is not survivable. It is time for Julie, for my daughter, for me, for all women to start speaking our needs. It is time to extract the resistance against women "needing" up by its roots—roots that are, in part, about our fear of not being liked—and give it a ceremonial burning. For women, and especially young women, the fear of losing our friends and ending up alone is the worst fate imaginable. We need the company of other females, but we need to wake up and realise that we need to know our needs more. We need to feel loved, appreciated, valued, heard and respected. We need to love, appreciate, value, listen to and respect ourselves. We need to feel confident in our ability to financially and emotionally take care of ourselves. We need to know that we can rely on the important people in our life. And we need to listen to our feelings of exhaustion, boredom and grumpy out-of-sorts. These feelings are our messengers. They are not signs of weakness or badness, as we have been led to believe. Being irritated or grumpy are important signals that tell us that something is wrong or out of balance.

The truth is that women cannot thrive, or be equal or empowered, if we do not need. *We cannot be everything to everyone, because if we try, we will be nothing to ourselves.* Without this knowing, we will become completely given-out. Anna, a client, had a wonderful image of herself as a sponge that soaked up everyone's issues and needs until she became completely saturated and full. To survive, we have to learn to become *everything to ourselves* first, to ask ourselves: *"What feels right for me and works for me too?"*

It took me a year to realise how it felt when a close friend accused me of being "too needy." I'd been too afraid of losing her friendship to examine how her accusation felt. So I did what I had learned to do. I swallowed her words and retreated into my "let me just focus on you" box.

I don't know what woke me up, but suddenly I heard my voice saying, "Of course I was bloody needy, I was in a terrible situation at that time!" Suddenly, I saw the context in which she had accused me of being "needy." It was just before my doctor signed me off work for six weeks with stress and exhaustion, when my body had told me I could no longer cope with a work culture defined by silence and invisibility. My fear of losing my friend had confused me at the time of her admonishment. But as I reflected on how I had behaved, I knew that I hadn't passed my responsibility for my problems onto her. Instead, I started to see how little space I had in this relationship, and that her definition of "You're too needy" was code for me not being available for her.

It was hard, in a good way, to wake up to how easily I switched myself off because my needs made me feel wrong, which then stopped me from recognising the code behind her accusation. Being needy meant I wasn't being nice, kind, helpful, and available. Claiming our needs is a simple prescription. It asks: *"What do I need?* What do I need in this situation? What do I need in this relationship?" Yet following through with this simple question is extremely hard. For many of us, the mere questioning challenges our family's, and society's, deeply held beliefs that women should nurture others and not themselves. It also slams straight up against the unacknowledged fear that if women start nurturing themselves, they will no longer be available or want to nurture others.

Nurturing ourselves is the only way to change our lives, our daughters' lives, and society's denial of women's needs and create a conversation that speaks our needs. For me, claiming my needs and learning to feel entitled to be *needy* was the only way to reverse the pattern of *needless* mothers and daughters that has, for too many generations, made women invisible and unnurtured in my family.

We need to have more of the kinds of conversations that my friend Barb and I had. We laughed with a strong feeling of comradeship about her brother calling her "selfish," then resolved to believe this was actually a good sign—that it indicated she was finally starting to think about herself and tuning into her antennae. We also resolved to support each other to keep hold of our hard-won self-focus. As women, we must support each other in those crucial moments when the criticism becomes too hard to sit with and not believe, too hard to push back and not own, and too hard to ignore and not have it change our behaviour.

Exercises to create the conversation that speaks my needs!

Take some time and write these two lists.

- Firstly, write down all the things you have done to take care of others during the last week. Don't leave anything out! Don't fall into the trap of underestimating what you do. If you hear yourself say, "That's nothing," write it down anyway.

- Then, write down all the things you've done in the last week to take care of yourself.

- Look at the two lists. Notice the difference in length, time commitment and substance. Notice the woman who is doing all the cooking, shopping, nursing, helping with homework, listening, birthday party planning, chauffeuring, helping out at school or the kids' club, or taking care of sick or elderly friends and family members. Notice the woman who is worried about how others are doing, building a career, trying to make a competent impression at work while juggling all her responsibilities.

- Ask yourself:

    1. Why am I doing all this? Am I doing this because it's right for me, or because I think I should?
    2. Why do I think I should? Where did I get that message? Who told me?
    3. What do I need for myself today? (Don't worry if the answers don't come immediately. When our voices have been switched off for a while, they need some time to get switched back on again.)
    4. How much time for myself do I have? (Time at work doesn't count. I tricked myself into thinking that. Work isn't the place to recharge your batteries.)
    5. Do I say what I need? If not, why not? Is there something within me that is stopping me from speaking my needs? Or, do I sense that my needs aren't welcome? Or both?
    6. Why am I still in relationships where my needs aren't valued?
    7. This question will require that you reflect on your family's history with female needs. Was there a conversation in your family that acknowledged women's needs? Did your mother and grandmother communicate their needs? If not, why not? If they did, how? What words and sentences did they use? Were they effective?

9: Claiming My Feelings and Anger

Women are wounded every time their anger is shushed,
criticised as unfeminine, and used as an excuse to
withhold love and understanding. – RH

Kate announced her arrival in my office with the words, "I didn't get angry so I wasn't aggressive" as she sat down heavily in her chair. She went on to describe how she was angry with her sister for expecting her to look after her two nieces without being asked. This wasn't the first time her sister had expected her to be on-call. She had performed child-minding services and various other jobs countless other times, without a please or thank you, or an enquiry as to whether she could, had the time, or was willing. Kate was also angry with herself. She again hadn't said no, or even complained. She had compliantly looked after her nieces without saying anything about how she was feeling used.

This had happened only a few days earlier, and initially she felt some relief that she had kept quiet and saved herself from feeling bad about being aggressive. But as she was thinking about coming to see me, her initial relief could no longer numb her anger about her sister's behaviour or her own inability to stand up for herself. She hated her fearful "wobbliness" that gagged her voice and made her time fair game for anyone who needed her. But she didn't know how to say no or voice her true feelings. All she knew to do was to talk herself out of feeling angry, even though this time she wasn't being very successful at it.

I knew all too well the confused fear Kate was describing. I can look back at times when I felt hurt and angry and said nothing. Instead of speaking, I sentenced myself to many hours, weeks, even months of ruminating over the event while I tried to find the words I had wanted to speak but didn't. A battle would rage inside me between feeling guilty for upsetting the person if I spoke my truth and honouring my feelings and needs: between fearing that my feelings would be dismissed, disliked or criticised and valuing my feelings and needs by not allowing others to place their value on them. Each time, I would resign myself to a battle like the one I had around my supervisor's dismissal of my needs. (See chapter 2 "Our Silenced Voices.")

I know that Kate and I aren't the only women who doubt the validity of our feelings. Countless women crumple away their feelings because they know they won't be welcome, heard or accepted. Kate's belief that being silent is the only way to avoid being aggressive describes the tragic picture of what it is like to be female in a silencing society. Her words show how much she had learned to believe that speaking her feelings, especially her anger, is bad. Like Kate, many of us are oblivious to how incorrect her statement is. We don't understand how self-harming it is to suppress our anger and turn it against ourselves as guilt, a guilt that is misplaced because being angry isn't a crime. Yet inside it feels as if somehow we must be wrong. When we don't have a place to have our anger heard and valued, we can trick ourselves into thinking we are bad because it is easier and safer. I see this happening in the stories countless women tell me. Their emotional disconnection, depression, low self-esteem and anxiety are all a direct result of suppressed anger. In that crumpled-away place, we learn to not feel or know our truth until slowly, feeling by feeling, we disconnect from ourselves and stop hearing our voices.

Why do we do this to ourselves? Why did Kate feel so uncomfortable about feeling angry about being used? Why did it take me the better part of a year to know how I felt about my friend's comment about being "too needy"? (See chapter 8 "Claiming my Emotional Needs") Why did Kate and I subject ourselves to the tormenting inner debate about whether we should or shouldn't speak? And why are women more concerned about hurting other people's feelings than how hurt we feel?

The answer to these questions is that we have internalised the messages that have taught women to believe our feelings have less value than how others feel about us. And we have internalised the expectation that, as women, we are to care more about what others need than our own needs. Speaking our feelings, especially when we're angry, feels scary and dangerous because it hits up against these two strongly held beliefs. The idea of speaking out invokes the many criticisms that keep women silent, including the "good-girl nice-woman" roles, and the myth that being assertive is only one step away from being aggressive. You see women being afraid every time they put their hand over their mouth when they speak. You can hear it in the tentative, unclear and uncertain way they speak, even though their words may be assertive. You hear it when they begin speaking with an apology. And in every time they change the subject, swallow their feelings and focus on what the other person is feeling. I became a master at this last one.

We can learn a lot about our silenced anger by looking at the relational world of adolescent girls. It would be a grave mistake to think that the conflict between adolescent girls is something unique and nothing to do with female silence. We would be missing the mirror image our girls are showing us of what happens in our relationships with ourselves and in our relationships with other women when there is no language, permission or words to speak our emotional truth.

Our girls are acting out and raging against being put to sleep like Sleeping Beauty. Their spirits don't like the message that good girls aren't entitled to feel, or be competitive and want to win, or to speak their feelings because someone else's feelings are more important. They hate learning that their strong feelings can damage their femininity and that they need to sugarcoat their feelings to preserve their "goodness." This creates a tension between their spirit's need to be known and the society that needs them to be quietly good, a tension impossible to manage, even though they try to manage it by creating a false, sweet calm on the surface that hides the anger and rage they're actually feeling underneath.

We have all seen it and sensed it. Girls learn to become masters at smiling too sweetly through unseen gritted teeth, while underneath they lash out with nastiness so well hidden, no one notices except girls themselves. They're lashing out at each other because they hate being silenced, but they have nowhere to tell the truth, and like Kate, they feel vulnerable, without permission to put limits on behaviour they don't want to accept from other people. It makes sense that some of them would resort to self-harm as a way of letting out the bad feelings or using pain as a check to confirm they still exist. Maybe this is also why they're so hurtful to each other. Does seeing that another girl hurts, or observing that their feelings have hurt someone else, somehow reassure them that their own feelings still exist?

Parents of adolescent girls know, too well, how destructive adolescent girls' relationships can be, how the bitchy, gossipy silent treatment and deliberate exclusion-and-inclusion power games can strip their daughter's self-esteem, whether they're in the in-group or the out-group. And all girls know how tenuous it is to be in the in-group. One wrong comment, one incorrect item of clothing, one wrong allegiance with an out-person means sudden expulsion. There are a number of good books that describe this well, including *Reviving Ophelia* by Mary Pipher, *Odd Girl Out* by Rachel Simmons, and *Queen Bees Wannabes* by Rosalind Wiseman.

Rachel Simmons warns in *Odd Girl Out:*

> *Denying those feelings [anger in particular] locks us away from ourselves and so from authentic relationships with others. Denying those feelings doesn't make them go away but somewhere else, leaving the people around us unsure of what we mean, who we are, and how we feel. Denying them takes us to a place others sense but do not see. It is a place no girl deserves to be.*[12]

No female deserves to be in this place. Silence takes us all to a dangerous place, one where we're emotionally disconnected from ourselves, not in control of our choices, and feeling invisible. It makes us asleep to ourselves, a slumber from which it can take a long time to awaken. It is the same crazy-making place where our screams of protest are ignored, leaving us feeling crazy-screaming and out of control. I wonder if this is what happened to mad Bertha in Charlotte Bronte's *Jane Eyre*. Suppressed feelings makes reality shift about in a way that makes it difficult to hold on to and trust. I hear women say that they feel the tension between speaking and silence as a tightness in their chest or an upset churning stomach.

Women usually awaken slowly to the knowledge that we too have rights, needs and feelings during our late twenties and thirties, continuing until our forties or fifties, often coinciding with our children leaving home. In a society threatened by the conversation that speaks women's feelings, we have to awaken ourselves. Unlike with Sleeping Beauty, no prince is going to kiss us awake. We have to awaken ourselves to the truth that silencing our feelings is sexist, cruel, and emotionally manipulative and abusive to the extreme, as the opening quote warns. We have to awaken to the knowing that our feelings are our lifeblood. They warn us when something is wrong, as Debra's did when she said no to someone who wasn't being respectful.

Debra, a friend, telephoned to tell me she had declined a rather lucrative teaching job. Even before she started the job, her soon-to-be boss was already being dismissive and disrespectful of her. He didn't turn up for their arranged meetings, and took ages to answer her questions, many of which he then dismissed as irrelevant. Though she knew this job would look good on her curriculum vita, she also realised that its entry would be won at a too high a cost to her self-worth.

I was impressed with how coolly Debra had decided this. She was angry, but she had kept her head together and never doubted her feelings. She didn't ruminate over the problem like I used to do. She knew she didn't like how the person's behaviour felt, and she simply said, "Thanks for the opportunity, but I have decided to not do the work, good-bye." In her certainty and assertiveness, I saw reflected the place all females deserve to be.

If we are to create that place for ourselves, for our daughters, for all women, it begins with daring to claim our feelings regardless of what anyone thinks. It begins with knowing that, without our feelings, we are not ourselves, and we are sentencing ourselves, our daughters, and each other to a half-life where we put up with silently trying to exist around everyone else. The bottom line in claiming this place for ourselves is just that: Only I can speak my needs, know my feelings and set the limits on what I will do and won't do. What I will accept and won't accept. Other people can choose to behave badly, try to guilt-trip me or criticise me into being silent, or subject me to silent treatment to blackmail me into being the way they need me to be. I have no control over how other people choose to behave. But I do have control over how I react to it and how I behave. I have control over what I choose to put up with, because I know I have a fundamental right to be in control of myself and to protect myself, and, like Debra, to say "No thanks" and walk way.

There is no magic formula to claiming our feelings. It is the same formula to claiming our needs. We simply have to learn to keep reminding ourselves to ask the question: *"What do I feel?"* Sometimes we won't know the answer straightaway, and that's okay. After years of having our feelings suppressed, it's reasonable for them to take their time coming out of hiding. And when we hear ourselves say, or someone else say, that we "should be," "must be" or "ought to be" feeling or doing something, beware! Those commands are warning bells, because "should be," "ought to be" and "must be" don't speak our truth. Rather, this is the language of our internal and socially condoned-and-learned bully that guilt-trips us into fitting in with others. Our job, then, is to hold fast to our truth and follow our feelings and needs.

Naomi Wolf says in *Fire with Fire,* "If you are a warrior for your rights, you must accept that some interests and people *should* lose. It's okay to harm a rapist in order to escape; it's okay to embarrass a discriminatory employer."[13] In keeping with this statement, when we look at history there are many women warriors who have put their foot down and said, "No, this isn't okay," and, "This inequality has to stop now, in my lifetime." It's important for all of us to realise that we are all warriors for ourselves. Being a warrior is all about having an active self-esteem that speaks and acts on our rights. Sometimes we need to shout and get angry, and sometimes, like Debra, we are required to say no with confidence. And when someone is slow at learning that we mean what we say, being a warrior for ourselves means not giving in. It means repeating our boundaries, like a broken record if required, until they are heard and respected.

For women to be fully visible, our anger needs to be celebrated. Anger is not our enemy. It is our healthy warning system that signals we're in danger. How we express our anger is what makes the difference. Using it to harm others or ourselves will only add to the cycle of violence. But when we use it to empower and protect ourselves, we are putting ourselves well on the journey of never again having to make a choice between being heard or being loved.

Exercises to say "No!"

Think of a recent moment when you said yes to something you didn't want to do, or didn't agree with. Ask yourself:

1. Why did I say yes?
2. What fears stopped me from saying no?
3. What beliefs gagged me from speaking my mind?
4. Whose feelings did I feel responsible for?
   Did my own come into the equation?

In addition to asking myself the above questions, buying time has helped me stay connected to myself when someone asks me to do something. My first response is to say: "I need to think about this, I'll get back to you soon."

Buying time can give you space to reflect on what you want to do. It can help you separate out your conditioning to take responsibility for someone else's needs and feelings rather than your own. This is time well spent because without it, you might be inclined to give in after the slightest pressure or guilt-tripping.

Buying time also gives you time to rehearse what you're going to say if the request isn't something you want to do. It gives you time to remind yourself that *"No" is a complete sentence.* That you don't have to go around the houses to explain your reasons for not doing something someone has requested, and that not respecting your no is extremely rude. This truth has been completely flipped about for women. It has been turned around to make women rude for saying no, rather than acknowledging how rude it is to dismiss and ignore someone who has said no. A woman's no is far too often heard as meaning "Maybe," or "She'll come around to it," or even "Yes." This twisted hard-of-hearing results in women being raped, taking responsibility for things they shouldn't and don't want to, and feeling angry because they have been completely ignored. The acceptability of suddenly changing the meaning of no to yes or maybe when it comes to women has to be challenged and changed. "No" has, and will always mean "No" for both men and women.

10: Claiming My Visibility and Value

Being truly heard, without having to scream,
is every woman's greatest longing. – RH

Vicky, a client, describes her invisibility as "soul-erasing loneliness." Her family and friends hardly ever ask her how she is or what she's doing, leaving her craving for people's attention. "I'm not talking about the quick 'how are you?' greeting that asks nothing more than a hello," she says. "I am talking about the people I care about asking me how I am because they want to know whether I am happy or sad, elated or grumpy. I want them to know the inside me, the things that are important to me, and have them ask how my day has been."

Vicky is voicing the depth of invisibility that far too many women are suffering from and believe is normal. She is describing a soul-erasing invisibility that has caring flowing as a one-way street: from herself to others. And when you don't know anything different, you feel you have no other choice than to try and survive without the relaxing nurturing of feeling heard. You haven't learned to question why you're the one who takes the time to ask how someone is, or who telephones just because you've been thinking about them, or visiting because you know someone's going through a bad time, while your telephone and doorbell remain ominously silent.

Invisible women tell me that their cravings to be known make them feel anxious, weak, needy, and powerless. They don't know how to become more visible, or how to make people notice them. Yet they also admit that being visible actually scares them. They don't know how to ask or receive, or how to behave when someone does notice them. This recognition is such a foreign experience for them, they don't know what to do with it. They describe being filled with self-doubt and self-criticism for being "needy."

What these women describe is the process of becoming emotionally starved. As they silence their emotional needs and comply with the expectation that women are the givers and not receivers, they are, bit by bit, travelling down the dangerous road of becoming invisible to themselves and emotionally starved. Emotionally starved females have learned to silence their ability to know what they feel and need, and what emotional food they need to feel nurtured. They become mute inside, and in the worst cases, not unlike those suffering from anorexia, feeling invisible and not nurtured becomes seductively familiar and normal. Yet, just like with eating disorders, the heart cannot survive without some attention and emotional feeding, and this lack sentences them to a daily existence of living in a state of uncertain anxiety, because survival is dependent on snatching attention and love wherever they can.

The symptoms of being emotionally starved are easy to spot once you know the signs. In some women you recognise it because they've withdrawn into silence, while others talk and talk and talk, hijacking conversations by telling story after story, because they're so afraid that if they're silent for a moment, they will disappear from view. Some women lash out in anger; others use more passive-aggressive ways to voice their anger and feel in control. You see it in women who become obsessive carers. They're the ones who need to be needed, and have learned to become visible through being helpful. For these women, the thought of saying no, even if they knew how, fills them with dread, because without their caring, they'll be faced with their invisibility.

You can recognise emotional starvation in mothers who neglect themselves whilst putting all their energy into caring for their children and family. They are the mothers who put off seeing the doctor when something's bothering them, but when their child has the first sign of a sniffle, they drop everything and take it to the doctor. They're also the mothers who look to their daughters and sons to feed them, to reflect back what a great mother they are. These are women who don't own their own value, so are looking to others to constantly show them they have value. Some women shop too much, drink too much, eat too much or too little, all in the hope of anaesthetising the pain of feeling unknown. Their pain surrounds them like a thick, suffocating cloud, especially during the evenings, when the distractions of the day have quietened down.

Emotionally starved women ignore critical, jealous, controlling, or emotionally and physically abusive behaviour because being emotionally starved can make even bad and abusive attention feel like love. They reframe abuse to mean, *Finally, someone actually likes me and wants to be with me.* I have heard women reframe their partner's constant criticism as meaning, *He must care a great deal about me, because he's putting effort into helping me improve myself.*

Being ignored, not enquired after or consulted, being unknown and unheard and having our requests reacted to with defensive anger and rejection leaves us emotionally hungry. Having to compete with the newspaper, television, sports and work commitments for time and attention cuts away at our self-worth while we put up with feeling second best. We stop knowing that love isn't meant to make us feel bad and that attention isn't meant to feel scary.

I used to overwork to switch off my emotional hunger. During my early forties, my body finally started to say "enough," speaking through a range of symptoms that all screamed to me that I was burnt-out. When my body forced me to stop, I suddenly had the space in which to recognise my cycle of anaesthetising my pain of being invisible. My cycle of overworking would start with me recognising how invisible I was feeling in some of my important relationships. But, because I didn't yet know how to speak about what I needed, or how to nurture myself fully, I didn't know how it felt to believe that I *could* feel heard, valued and cherished, and then set boundaries with those who didn't reflect that value back to me. Lacking that knowledge, I would try to dull my feelings by working until I was exhausted. Having reached exhaustion, I could then finally give myself the permission to take care of myself. Yet as soon as I felt a little better, the anxiety of not feeling confident in my own value rose up again, sending me back to work to repeat the cycle.

My other anaesthetising behaviour that switched off my inner yearnings was to completely focus on the other person's needs. I believe my mother and grandmother had the same cycles. Overworking was revered in my family as noble behaviour, and for women, selfless caring was the only way to get valued.

Vicky discovered her cycle of coping with her emotional starvation and hunger during her early twenties. Vicky, a soft-spoken, compliant, sensitive, hollow-looking young woman, had learned to switch off her needs in her relationships, to anaesthetise her yearnings by starving, bingeing, and obsessing about food and how empty or full her stomach was. She had been using food to control her feelings since adolescence. It all started when she suddenly learned to believe that feeling hungry was a sign that she was in control of her life. Slowly, hunger began to feel seductively good, until her obsession about food and how little she could eat became so acute and all encompassing, it gave her no time or space to recognise that her emotional hunger was speaking through her connection with food.

Vicky's relationship with food was, in fact, a metaphor for her relationships with her parents, boyfriend and herself. Her parents were emotionally unavailable to her. Her father's attention was taken up with work; her mother was depressed and emotionally lost. Her boyfriend demanded a lot of time and attention from her. Vicky was the one who did all the listening-to, caring about, and doing what others wanted. She didn't know how to emotionally feed herself, have her voice heard, or set protective boundaries that spoke clearly that to be in a relationship with her meant valuing her, knowing her, and respecting her.

Vicky, Jill (See chapter 3 "Taught to Be Silent") and I had all learned to switch ourselves off as a way of coping with our lack of value and lack of conversation about how to nurture ourselves and ask to be nurtured. We didn't know how else to respond to people's demands as they echoed loudly in our hollow emptiness. But switching off emotional hunger doesn't work. All hunger demands feeding before it will go away, and emotional hunger is no exception. It has a voice of its own that will find a way to speak, if not always directly. For me, it was my body that first woke me up. Vicky woke up by becoming angry about her boyfriend's selfishness. And Jill became angry and started to wonder why she was feeling so alone and unseen. All of us feared that our invisibility and loneliness was telling us that we weren't worth knowing. But slowly, we all learned to see what a big fat lie that was.

Being emotionally starved leaves us not in our right-minds. *Our relationships are a mirror reflection of our relationship with ourselves and our belief about what we're worth.* Emotionally starved women are in danger of attracting and creating relationships in which they are invisible and emotionally starved.

But before we all start blaming ourselves and all women for creating our own invisibility and second-sex status, we have to first understand that if we blame women for attracting their own invisibility, we'll only be telling half the story and blaming the victims of female invisibility. *True healing requires us to understand how we have been taught to be invisible before we can begin the process of taking responsibility for our invisibility.* We need to tell the story of how our female souls have been wounded by the denial of our voices and the dictates of female "goodness" and "niceness" by the assumption that, as a female, a mother, a daughter, we're somehow assumed to be less valuable, less equal, less requiring of nurturing and being fully known, because our value is only seen through the caring we do for others.

Getting back into our right minds requires us to create a new normal for ourselves. We have to awaken to the possibility that we are valuable, equal, and just like everyone else in our family and the world, that we have souls and needs that require nurturing, feeding and listening to. We are the only ones who can create this new normal for ourselves. *We have the power and right to create relationships that reflect this new normal, relationships that nurture us as much as we do the nurturing.*

A normal that never questions that need for nurturing is a two-way street. I knew I was on my way to creating this new normal when I didn't switch off my feelings or focus away from myself when a friend completely dismissed my boundaries and then criticised me for reminding her of them. This time, I knew straightaway that I was in a relationship in which my feelings had no voice, and if she did not hear how I was feeling, it was time to walk away. My mirror of what I was learning to believe as possible was changing as my antennae's ability to pick up my internal signals grew stronger. The more value I gave myself, the more I saw that if I allow someone to treat me badly, I was holding up a mirror in which I saw reflected my own inner lack of value. That if I accept being silenced, criticised, rejected or ignored, I am saying that this is okay because I am not worth better treatment.

I am grateful for my relationship with my parents-in-law, because they gave me a great lesson in valuing my voice and feelings. For years, I tried to speak to them about what I was feeling about their behaviour toward me. I felt they could only see me as their son's wife who was in service to him, and to their grandchildren, just as I had watched my mother, grandmother, and mother-in-law be. I didn't feel valued as my own person, and felt stifled against an unspoken rule that any discussion about relationships was taboo. I was also afraid to speak. Experience had taught me that the punishment for breaking this rule was to invoke their anger and the unspoken energy within the family that I was behaving in an unacceptable way. But that wasn't the only reason I was afraid to speak. Their punishment reflected my own uncertainty as to whether I had the *right* to speak. I didn't value myself enough, and this made me need their approval too much.

My relationships started to change as I slowly returned my antennae back to myself, and became more solid about knowing that any relationship in which I felt silenced, not enquired after, criticised, ignored, or taken for granted is not a relationship worth being in. These relationships no longer reflected who I felt I was and deserved to be. I started to feel more nurtured as I learned to speak my needs and feelings with more confidence. I was coming out of hiding and no longer sentencing myself to a life of soul-crushing invisibility. I was learning to understand the power and right I had to claim my responsibility for my visibility, and to believe that *I am only as invisible as I allow myself to be.*

I don't know what finally switched this belief on for me in a way that no one, not even my parents-in-law, could switch off. One day I just felt I had had enough with my parents-in-law's angry punishment. I decided that day to believe that if they were to enjoy knowing me, being around me, and seeing me, they were going to have to listen to me without anger. It became a very firm boundary for all my relationships. I no longer felt afraid or intimidated by their anger, or needing of their approval. I knew without doubt that *they* were the ones missing out, not I, because the relationship they were offering me was one that was sentencing me to soul-destroying invisibility.

And now, being in my right mind, I know how to ask for support and feed myself. How different would things have been if I had been in my right mind when my professor said to me, "I don't know if you know this, but you are very good at this." He was remarking on his research-and-statistics class, which I was taking. I remember being stunned by his comment. I didn't know what to say, so I dismissed it because the mirror he was holding up to me didn't fit the reflection I was expecting to see. I didn't think I was good at research, so I dismissed and forgot his comment. What different paths and choices might I have made if I *had* recognised myself in his mirror, or had enough sense of my own worth to take on his comment, his nourishing gift he was offering me that day, as a truth.

I wish this kind of clear-eyed knowing for all girls and women. Like Tanya, who said, "It is amazing what women can do when we feel supported." She had the right mind to gather around herself all the support she needed during her home-birth experience. And because of this, she believes, the birth went beautifully and the experience ended up being a life-changing, empowering moment for her, as I am sure it was for all those who had the privilege of witnessing it. In the months following the birth, she continued to ask for support. As I sat next to her while she was feeding her tiny daughter, she said, "All I have to do is take care of myself and take care of my baby." Her partner was home and doing everything else, and she was fully able to let it all go. I marvelled at how truly in her right mind she was at this time in her life. She was in touch with herself. She knew what she was feeling and needing, what was possible and not possible, and she never questioned or criticised her knowing. She didn't have to be anxious about grabbing time or attention, because she owned her time and was confident that attention and love was always available for her. What a wonderful start she had given herself and her new daughter!

Exercise in speaking my value and visibility

Think about your important relationships. How do you feel about them? What messages are you ignoring about your place and value in your relationships? Ask yourself:

1. Am I putting up with a lack of concern and enquiry? Why?
2. Do I feel anxious when I want to say how I am feeling? Is this because there's something within me making me feel and behave as if I am less entitled, or is there something in the relationship that is silencing me, or both?
3. Do I feel seen and known by those that matter to me?
4. Am I trying to be seen and heard in relationships where someone is clearly not listening?
5. Have I ever experienced feeling rejected and invisible in a relationship, especially an important relationship? How did that feel? What wounding belief did I take away from that experience? How is that belief affecting me now and continuing my invisibility?

11: Claiming My Availability for Myself

Unavailable women are scary! Unavailable mothers are dangerous! When women and mothers address their needs, all sorts of fears get unearthed in themselves and in others. – RH

It is hard to hold on to what we feel we need or what we know is best for us, without wavering, when being unavailable makes some people angry, scared and a little crazy toward us. People don't like it when women, especially mothers, aren't available, or seem too focused on themselves. You can smell the fear against women being unavailable in the air. Kids act-up as soon as they sense that Mum's attention is diverted. Suddenly they desperately need her when she's on the telephone, in the bathroom, or having some time-out. But it's not just kids who don't like it when Mother's attention is somewhere else. Grown men and women can also play-up when women aren't available.

Being unavailable or setting your own boundaries, or claiming the right to follow your passion and live the life you desire, is still seen as unthinkable for women. I experienced my entire counselling service, which interestingly was an all-female department, turning against me because I refused to take on someone else's job as well as my own. Our secretary wanted to go part-time, but instead of hiring someone else to job-share with her, the idea was suggested that we all help out with secretarial duties during the days she wasn't working. When I refused because I wasn't contracted or trained to do secretarial work and I was already stressed and overloaded in my own job, my colleagues didn't like it one bit. They responded with a wall of criticism, accusing me of being "unsupportive," "selfish," "not a team player," and their entire attitude was, "How dare you ignore what everybody else wants."

My support of our secretary's plan to go part-time and the reasonableness of why I said no got lost in the criticism. They also didn't see how their plan degraded the importance of our secretary's skills and job, giving the unspoken if real impression that they felt "anybody can do her job." All they heard was that I wasn't available to help out. This was a department that wasn't being treated with a lot of respect within the organisation. Assertiveness by the department wasn't tolerated, and also it seems, not within the service. I was expected to go along with their collective fear around asking for what they needed, which in this case was a half-time secretary to fill in the other secretary's now-missing hours.

Though it was very difficult at the time, I am glad I stuck my neck out. It helped me find the motivation to leave that job and department. Voices that speak against us when we're only doing what is right, nurturing, and protective for us need to be ignored.

When I announced that I had been accepted into a master's degree programme, my mother's only comment was, "And who is going to look after your children?" My father-in-law reacted angrily, asking me, "And what about John's doctoral studies?" Though the lack of support hurt, I knew enough to know these voices needed to be ignored.

In all fairness, it's hard to stay available to ourselves when we aren't liked for doing it. It's hard to resist the pressures to give in, to silence our inner screams of protest, and to chop ourselves up into more acceptable smaller pieces. I hear countless women admit that even though they regard themselves as being assertive and knowing their minds, they change their voices, talk themselves down, or just don't say anything out of fear of not being liked or being criticised. Our learned silence bullies women into not cancelling family gatherings we're expected to cater for. We martyr on because we worry more about not spoiling it for everyone else and appearing selfish. We ignore our body screaming at us to stop, even though I remember time after time feeling even worse afterward, because I knew I hadn't listened to myself. Again.

Sue, a friend, told me how she downsized to a much smaller home to give herself the excuse to not look after her newly widowed father. Her gut instinct was telling her she'd had enough of caring for others now that her children had left home. She wanted space for herself. But her learned silence protested loudly, telling her it wouldn't be right for her to keep a big house all to herself and say no to looking after her father. It told her she had to reduce her living space before she was entitled to say no. And her relatives all joined in the chorus with how selfish she was with "all this space and time," because it suited them to have Sue look after their father.

Why do we all do this? Why do we stop being available for ourselves so easily? Because the universal fear, one conveniently backed up by many religious and sexist philosophies that see women as God-ordained carers, has infected us. We have learned, as my grandmother did, to think that being available, even if it means not being available for ourselves, is normal and "a woman's lot." It has taught us to consider others' needs more highly than our own, even if that leaves us feeling invisible, disconnected and emotionally starved. But we must resist! Because if we don't, we're in very real danger of losing touch with our life-affirming scream that flashes an unavoidable warning sign of danger when we're about to neglect ourselves by giving into the collective fear of not going along with other's wishes or being unavailable. We must resist because it begs the question, *"Why is it okay for females to live lives in which they aren't available for themselves?"*

Andrea was a woman in her late twenties who had been infected by the thinking that she was responsible for her mother's happiness, to the point in which she was seriously harming her own life and happiness. She came to see me because she was depressed and unsure as to how to make her mother respond to her in a kindly, respectful way. Andrea had been struggling with her mother's bitterness and criticism since her adolescence. What she described is, sadly, a common theme for daughters of mothers who haven't been given the permission to claim their own lives. Her mother had started to criticise Andrea during her adolescence because she couldn't bear to see her daughter embark on a life she couldn't have for herself. Her mother had spent her life in service to her family and everyone around her, never feeling entitled to follow her own passions and desires or being available to nurture her own life.

Andrea too had learned to criticise herself and doubt her own needs and passions. She was convinced that her mother's criticism was true, and all she had to do was try harder and be nicer, and hopefully her mother's heart would melt. Over the weeks of talking through her feelings and relationship with her mother, Andrea came to see that there was nothing wrong with her. She started to very tentatively set small boundaries with her mother, and eventually she learned to disconnect her self-worth, and her right to her own life, from her mother's cutting comments. Andrea stopped trying to get her mother's attention and goodwill and only engaged with her when she wanted to, and then only for the length of time she could manage.

It was wonderful to hear how her mother's behaviour also changed along with Andrea's growth in self-worth and strength to demand to have herself and her boundaries respected. Her mother stopped being critical and started to be genuinely pleased to see her when she visited. One day, her mother's heart did melt. She suddenly broke down and told her daughter the story of her painful lost unfulfilled dreams, and of how cold her own mother had been to her. Andrea had never heard her mother's story before, and hearing it made her love her mother with a new depth of understanding. She knew that her mother's jealous criticism, though not okay, came from a very painful place, one that had nothing to do with Andrea.

Andrea's depression melted away. She stopped being like a frozen rabbit in the headlights whenever her mother or anyone else was angry or critical of her. By having the courage to claim her rights and needs and no longer put up with bad behaviour from her mother, she healed herself and her relationship with her mother, and found a way to be respected in all her relationships. In short, Andrea became available to herself.

In *The Wisdom of Menopause*, Christiane Northrup describes that during perimenopause, women can come to a place where we no longer put up with or tolerate inequality, injustice or not being tuned into ourselves. She says:

> *It may not feel like a rescue at the time, but the clarity of vision and increasing intolerance for injustice and inequity that accompany the perimenopause changes are a gift. Our hormones are giving us an opportunity to see, once and for all, what we need to change in order to live honestly, fully and healthfully in the second half of our lives. This is the time when many women stop doing what I call "stuffing"—stifling their own needs in order to tend to everybody else's. Our culture expects women to put others first, and during the childbearing years most of us do, no matter the cost to ourselves. But at midlife we get the chance to make changes, to create lives that fit who we are—or, more accurately, who we have become.*[14]

Though it is wonderful that our bodies help us in our journey to becoming available to ourselves, why do we have to wait until our perimenopause? Why do we have to wait until we are over halfway through our life before we can claim our life? Don't we need to have access to our needs, rights and life during the first half as well as the second?

During her research for her book on issues women face as we enter our second adulthood, Suzanne Braun Levine discovered that the vast majority of women felt, with hindsight, that the cost of self-neglect was too high.

> *The rewards of being able to tune into another person's*
> *needs—and sometimes to answer them—are many,*
> *as we know; but the cost to our own needs can be high.*
> *When the women I talked to reviewed what had been*
> *lacking in their first adulthood, self-nurturing moved*
> *to the top of the list.*[15]

I cannot help but wonder how different menopause would be for us if the battle for ourselves is no longer a battle. Will we still get flushed with anger and cranky from having nothing left for ourselves? Harriet Lerner highlights that anger is an "inevitable" response when we "give in and go along". She warns that we are setting ourselves up for feeling angry when we ignore ourselves and live as if keeping "nice" in our relationships is more important than taking care of ourselves and being ourselves.[16]

If we add half-a-lifetime of stored anger to our hormone-driven perimenopausal anger, I cannot help but wonder how different our perimenopause could be if we didn't have half-a-life of stored anger to vent.

My passionate hope for all women, for all our daughters and granddaughters, is that we create a new motto, a new homecoming normal, one in which we know that *if it feels bad, it is bad, which makes it bad for us.* I wish for my daughter, for all daughters, that they don't have to wait until their body rescues them, because they will have learned how to come home to themselves right from the start.

Exercises in being available to ourselves

Ask yourself:

1. What do I say to myself under my breath when I am tired?
2. What is my body telling me?
3. What messages have I been ignoring?
4. What do I know is best for me? Answer this without any "yes buts."
5. Women's instincts have been rejected and silenced for generations. They are labelled as unscientific, unreliable, and affected by fluctuating hormones. What voices have I rejected as crazy, unreliable or hormonal?
6. What conditions do I need to help me hear my instinct more clearly?
7. What do I need to do every day to help me start to listen to myself?
8. Can I give myself five minutes of quiet each day? If not, why not?
   What am I saying about my relationship with myself if I'm not worth five minutes each day?
   Especially when I compare it with the time I give to other relationships.

Of all the women who speak about their journey home to themselves, they unanimously say that solitude, time with themselves, is crucial. Time with ourselves is a human essential, and especially a female essential with our relational wiring, our emotional starvation, our socialisation to care, and our antennae tuned away from our inner voices. At first, when I suggest this to clients, the thought of being alone terrifies them. This is especially true if they have lost their ability to tune into themselves. It feels too much like being alone, which in a way is telling the truth. Being by ourselves and hearing our inner silence brings home how lost we really are. But gradually, if you persevere, you will slowly tune into the whispers that have been there all along. You will begin to experience your time by yourself differently as you start to understand that being by yourself is not being alone, it is being with yourself.

If the thought of being by yourself terrifies you, start small. Start with only five minutes, and gradually you will tune into yourself and be able to increase your time of solitude.

Reflect on your relationships and ask:

1. When have I felt ignored, silenced or criticised?
2. How did I react?
   Did I believe that the criticism was true?
3. Did I say anything?
   If so, what?
   Did it feel good to say it?
   If not, why not?
4. What needs or feelings did/do I ignore?
5. What do I need to do to reclaim my needs and feelings?
6. Do I have a pattern of certain needs or feelings being invisible in my relationships?
7. Do I need to say anything to the person/people who mistreated me?
8. What is their behaviour saying about how they value me?
9. What beliefs about myself do I need to change to feel more visible?
10. What conversations do I need to start having in my relationships to feel more visible?

12: Claiming and Healing My Wounds

*If I focus on what hasn't been and what isn't,
I will miss out on what is and what can be. I will miss out
on the gifts of wisdom and inner strength
that my wounding has taught me. – RH*

The only antidote against silence is to speak. The only way to heal our soul and claim our self-worth, to avoid a dead-zone from forming around our hearts, is to tell our story. To talk and write until you have talked and written it out of your system. Until it is done and you don't need to read from those pages again. Find good people who will listen and empathise with you, people who will sit with you while you cry and who do not need to change your feelings or fix them. People who will give you all the time and space you need for your journey back to yourself.

I have found through my work with women that just telling our story, though an essential first ingredient, isn't enough in itself. We also need to expose how the wounding has affected our self-worth and how it has disempowered us. It is important to find people who will help you retrieve yourself, pull you back from those moments when you lost touch with yourself. Find someone who will walk with you on your journey of claiming the voices you didn't get to speak while you extract your self-worth from events and experiences in which you ended up feeling shamed and blamed. This journey will also help you to understand who you are, how your history has shaped you, and how your particular sensitivities and personality type both protected you and made the mistreatment particularly harmful for you.

This is the journey my clients need me to witness, as well as the journey I have been on. I know all too well those moments during the journey when we fear that our pain is going to be permanent, even debilitating. But I also know, having come through them, that when it feels like it is the darkest and nothing seems possible, a breakthrough comes. I would suddenly see something I hadn't seen before, an insight or a different way of understanding something, something that would come from somewhere and bring with it the power to ease and heal, along with a surge of strength and sureness I hadn't dreamed possible. These miraculous light-bulb moments would come through a word someone said, or a line in a book I happened to pick up. Or suddenly, I would hear myself say something important as if I had spoken this truth for the first time. Often, these moments came when I was busy with the ordinary tasks of the day: having a shower, or doing the dishes, or glancing out the window and noticing something outside that helped me recognise something in myself that had been hidden before.

I have learned, through my own journey and through the courage of the wonderful women whose journeys I have been privileged to midwife, that true healing doesn't require us to physically hear the person who has harmed us say "sorry." I'm not saying we have to forgive or ignore someone's harmful behaviour. Of course, in order to heal that relationship, we certainly do need them to own their harm. But our healing of our relationship with ourselves and our self-worth doesn't depend on someone else's growth or honesty. We have the power to claim that for ourselves, whether we hear "sorry" or not.

It was a fantastic moment when I realised that *my mother's silence and my father's inability to claim his relationship with me said nothing about my worth.* I suddenly saw that they weren't being rejecting, abandoning and smouldering in angry silence because I deserved it, had asked for it, or needed to be punished.

They behaved in this way because of their own reasons: reasons that can only be found in their own experiences of being abandoned, rejected, and silenced.

Realising that even though, at times, my parents' silent treatment felt very personal, that it isn't, felt like a ton-weight lifting off my shoulders. I finally felt free: free to no longer be a victim to their behaviour. Dad died many years ago, so I will never get a "sorry" from him. But even though Mum is alive, I don't have to wait and hope that she will say "sorry" and change before I can let go of the hurt and claim my life. If I held out for the "sorry" I needed, I would never be free and always be at the mercy of her silence. My self-worth would forever be tied to her behaviour, so I wouldn't own it. Instead, I would be sentencing myself to having my self-worth jolted about like a roller coaster. I would feel okay if she spoke to me—which was dependent on my behaving how she wanted me to behave—and then plummet when the inevitable silence would descend, which I also had no control over. In short, I would be a puppet, and my need for approval would give her control over my strings.

It was strangely liberating to no longer feel dependent on my parents' understanding of themselves and me before I could feel free. I could heal myself and set myself free, so I was no longer affected by and weighed down by Mum's behaviour: behaviour that, in the past, had the power to knock me off-centre. Suddenly, her silent rejection moved away from me. It was no longer staring back at me, telling me that I was worthless. Instead, it was telling me the story of her emotional disconnection and of her dead zones, all of which had damaged her ability to see and hear not just herself but also her daughter.

This insight helped me understand the truth that *you cannot give what you do not own yourself.* For Mum to be able to hear or see me, or recognise how her behaviour affected me, she must first have had to experience being heard and understood herself, by her own parents. Sadly, she didn't receive enough empathy and listening. Family secrets, a concentration-camp experience during the war that was taboo to talk about, and maybe other experiences that I don't know about, have shut her down and created a dead zone. Dad too had experiences that created a wall around him. His father died when he was six, and as a result, he lost most of his family when he and a few of his brothers were sent to grow up in what sounded like an emotionally depriving and punitive boys' home. Like Mum, he didn't talk about his childhood. Both my parents learned how to survive by shutting down, and my father learned to live by the motto "Peace at all cost." He didn't learn that there is *no peace for anyone who feels they have to keep quiet in order to keep the peace.*

Understanding why someone behaves in a hurtful manner aids forgiveness. I don't agree with the school of thought that expects us to "Forgive and forget." To me, it sounds more like silencing someone's experiences and anger through the dictate that we shouldn't blame anyone. This type of forgiveness cannot facilitate healing; it is the voice of silence that is invested in denying women's experiences. It also makes us feel responsible for someone else's behaviour. Forgiveness, to me, means no longer feeling influenced by the power of the hurtful experiences. It means that I am feeling separate from my parents' silent treatment and not limited by it, choked by it, or cloaked by it. I remember that for years I felt cloaked by the feeling that I was an orphan. The feeling of being rejected and discarded hung around me; I breathed it in with every pore. I don't feel that anymore. Feeling orphaned is no longer at the centre of my being. I have moved on, and as a result feel more whole and real and in the centre of my life.

Forgiveness also requires getting angry. Without our anger, we won't feel what has happened to us and what we have lost and needed and didn't get. We need to get angry to understand that our needs remained whether they were met or not. Anger helps us push back the responsibility of the hurtful behaviour to those who perpetrated it. Anger is an essential part of mourning and it shakes free our fear and guilt. Before I was ready to open my eyes and see that my mother and grandmother also didn't get mothered, I had to mourn never having the mothering and mother-daughter relationship I needed. Having cried out my story, I can see that Mum couldn't give what she never received and what she couldn't do for herself. Even though she'll always be responsible for her behaviour, she also did the best she could from her unrecognised empty place. Mothering from an empty place, from a starved place, is close to impossible.

Switching off or denying our anger creates its own scars. When I switched off my anger at Dad when he said he could no longer come and visit me because it made Mum angry, I created an extra wounding for myself. My suppressed anger stopped me knowing that I was feeling very hurt, and it also stopped me from telling someone what happened and receiving the empathy I needed. If I had been angry, I would've passed back the shame of that moment to Dad straightaway. I wouldn't have carried it with me as a silent, toxic shame for years afterwards, fearing that he said no because of me, rather than the real reason, which was all about him. Talking about it would've helped me work through my feelings and come to understand that even though I know why he said no, it wasn't okay. It would've helped me to see how silent treatment is the worst kind of manipulative behaviour, because it creates a vacuum in which nothing is possible, since it kills all possibility for communication, understanding, healing and connection.

In spite of all this, in spite of the passage of time, I had to *pass back the shame and hurt so that I didn't pass it forward.* As I have described with my female legacy, emotional disconnection and starvation is easily passed on from mother to daughter when there's no conversation in the family that speaks a woman's emotional needs. You also see the same pattern happening when women repeat their childhood experience of being with men who are abusive and controlling. This happens when a woman hasn't paused to examine how her relationship with her father and mother has affected her. She hasn't extracted her self-worth from where it was lost during the violence or control she experienced and witnessed, and then passed back the shame to those that were controlling or violent. Until she does that, she won't know what real love feels like. She won't be able to read the danger signs, and she will misinterpret violence or emotional control as love. And as she repeats this pattern in her life, it will be passed forward, not just in her life, but in her children's lives, because they too are being exposed to the same experiences she was.

I saw history repeating itself in my children's eyes during our first Christmas morning in America. Ben and Olivia were sitting on the floor opening their presents, and as they were coming to the end of gathering in their loot, they both suddenly stopped and said, "Where are the presents from Oma and Opa? Haven't they sent us anything? Why haven't they sent us anything?"

I didn't know what to say. What could I say? As I looked into their faces, I saw their eyes looking hurt and confused. I saw them wondering if they had done something wrong to cause their grandparents to not send them anything for Christmas. My heart constricted. The hurt I saw in their eyes was familiar to me, a hurt I had so wanted to spare them from knowing. Yet here, on this Christmas morning, I knew I hadn't spared them, and maybe at some level, couldn't.

I tried to explain to them that this wasn't their fault. That my mother was angry with me for leaving New Zealand, and that she was struggling to come to terms with me doing things she couldn't control. I think they understood in their four- and seven-year-old minds. But for me this wasn't over; it had only just begun. This was another wake-up call, for me to deal with and completely own my hurt about my parents' silence. I had to do it for myself so I wouldn't continue to accept emotionally manipulative behaviour in my relationships. And by claiming this new normal for myself, I would be giving my children a different picture from what I had learned to accept. The silence had to stop with me, and not continue as being an okay way of relating.

Exercises to heal my wounds

My journey to claiming and healing my wounds has followed the stages of emotional slavery to emotional liberation that Marshall Rosenberg outlines in his book *Nonviolent Communication: A Language for Life.*[17] He describes stage one as emotional slavery, where we see ourselves responsible for other people's feelings. Stage two he calls the obnoxious stage (not a title I like), in which we feel angry and we no longer want to be responsible for other people's feelings. When I see women get to that stage, it's time to rejoice because they are on their way to claiming their voices. It is a wonderful stage where we stop caring about what others think of us as our antennae starts to focus back in on us. And stage three is the emotional liberation stage where we take responsibility for our intentions and actions.

When I was in stage one, I felt all I could do was put up with the silent treatment. During my twenties, I behaved like a battered daughter. I would put up with the silence, never daring to think I could question it. I went back time and time again, each time hoping that this time it would be different. I spent years trying to find the key that would unlock my parents' silence and enable them to let me in: the key I hoped would soften their hearts and change their behaviour so I would no longer feel invisible. But nothing worked. I didn't realise then that nothing was going to work, because the situation wasn't within my power to change.

I think that writing a letter to my parents helped me move to stage two. In this letter, I used all the non-judgemental and assertive "I language" I could find to explain how I was feeling and what I needed from them. I think a part of me was hoping this letter would be the key, but a larger part wrote the letter for myself. I needed to speak to them, and writing a letter was the best way of communicating what I needed to say; the process gave me time to think and communicate clearly my thoughts and feelings. I also needed to challenge my fear of speaking my truth and invoking their anger; I had to do something to make it worse, in order to break the spell the threat of silence had over me.

Through my work with women, I have come to believe that speaking to those who have hurt us is extremely important. Sometimes the person is dead, which makes it more difficult. But I marvel at the creative ways my clients come up with to find a way of speaking. Some of them write letters, others do it through music, and others take a memorable trip or speak at a graveside. I myself have had mock funerals and spoken poems to the sea, after which I throw the words into the sea, hoping the sea will do its magic and wash away my pain. Whenever I discuss with a client what it is she needs to do, I think it's important to process what they are hoping to achieve for themselves, for their relationships, and if there are any negative consequences. If a family or relationship has rules of silence, then speaking will always challenge that rule. It is important that the client is not emotionally or physically hurt by the experience. Her safety is paramount, and some people will do anything to keep the truth or their responsibility from being voiced. Yet, having said that, I don't think we should keep quiet if speaking will make the relationship worse. I don't believe there is "peace at any cost," because the cost of silence is far too great. So with safety in mind, finding a way to speak, whether directly or indirectly or through creative means, is important—to speak with the goal to break the bonds of her own internalised silence. So that even if the person who has harmed her doesn't acknowledge their harmful behaviour, she knows it happened, she knows it wasn't okay, and she knows it will always be their shame to carry.

Getting angry is part of stage two, because *the truth does set you free*. Silence needs to be attacked with sound. We have to get angry to challenge and dissolve our toxic shame and place responsibility with those who did the deed. Anger helps us to relearn that how we have been treated wasn't okay. I also think that for women, something physical can help in the process of pushing back the secrets and silence that have misshapen us. I have found kickboxing is a wonderful way of punching back. I imagine the person who has hurt me standing in front of me while I punch and kick, and at the end of the class I feel much better.

Stage three comes about gradually, the more real and precious we become to ourselves. It can also come after the final straw, the last mistreatment that finally pushes you on. I had such a push during a telephone conversation after years of no contact. I spent the conversation listening to my mother talk and talk about herself, and each time I tried to tell her about me or my children, or talk about our respective silence, she either froze out the conversation or changed the subject. Something inside me clicked. This was a good click, a light-bulb click that cleared my vision and helped me know I wasn't going to get heard, and that it was up to me to set and reinforce my boundaries. The click gave me permission to protect myself from not having my feelings acknowledged or being enquired after. It helped me own the fact that being invisible knocks me off-centre, and that this isn't good for me. It helped me recognise that *normal relationship rules still apply, even with mothers*: When someone is harmful, we need to create a way to protect ourselves.

I like the following mantra that I heard at a workshop facilitated by Caroline Myss: *"There is only one choice to make—do what will increase my energy and self-worth and don't do what will deplete my energy and self-worth."*[18]

My relationship with myself had become too valuable to risk losing!

Ask yourself:

1. What shameful and negative beliefs do I believe about myself?
2. What incident(s) made me believe this about myself?
3. What needs have been ignored or violated?
4. What do I need now to help me challenge and change these negative beliefs so I learn to see the false truth they hold?
5. What do I need now to help meet the needs that were shamed and ignored?

6. What do I need to say to help push back the shame and responsibility for the wounding behaviour?

7. Am I currently in a wounding relationship or situation? Why?

8. Am I using my wounds to get attention or diminish my responsibility for myself?
   If so, what do I need to do to help me become more responsible for myself?

9. What choices am I making that are decreasing my energy and self-worth?
   Why am I making these choices?

10. What choices do I need to make to increase my energy and self-worth?
    What is stopping me from making these choices?

13: Claiming My Body

I rarely meet women who don't battle with their appetite. Most women misjudge their hunger. They don't eat when they're hungry or stop when they're full. They criticise themselves for eating what they like, and then starve to pay penitence for their loss of control and wanting. And when they look at their reflection in the mirror, they struggle to love what they see. Instead, thoughts of disgust and wanting the reflection to be different flood their minds as they look away. Most women, and I include myself here, feel conflicted and confused about our appetite. We spend our lives yo-yoing between eating too much and eating too little, never really trusting our appetites or even knowing what hunger and feeling satisfied really feel like.

Looking at the messages that women are bombarded with everyday, it isn't surprising that women struggle with their appetite. Christiane Northrup points out in *Women's Bodies, Women's Wisdom*:

> *Our entire culture promotes dietary schizophrenia.*
> *Women's magazines tell us how to "Take 10 Pounds*

> *Off Fast" in the same issue in which they print "Five
> Chocolate Recipes Your Family Will Love You For."
> An insatiable market looks weekly for the next diet,
> because the real issues underlying why they overeat
> [and under eat] are never addressed.* [19]

Yet our battle with our appetite is screaming something
important. It is as if, in our ambivalence with our appetite, we're
making physical the lack of conversation that speaks our
emotional needs. Our confusion with our appetite is saying the
same thing that our confusion to ask, to be given, and to nurture
ourselves is saying. It makes sense that if we don't know how to
feed ourselves emotionally, or if we don't feel entitled to feed
ourselves or be fed, we will then be unsure about how to feed
ourselves physically. After all, how can we hear our body's signals
if we aren't taught to speak what we need?

Women are surrounded by a kind of body madness, a powerful
madness that takes over our minds and turns our daughters into
waif-like adolescents and adult women into shamed diet-obsessed
body haters. A madness that makes us see ourselves through what
the culture dictates as beautiful through its agents—the fashion,
cosmetic, diet, weight-loss, fitness, and cosmetic surgery
industries. Even though I know this, I can still feel its grip. I still
have to shake myself to not listen too closely to their messages,
and must remind myself that their survival and profit is
completely dependent on women (and men) feeling dissatisfied
with their bodies. These industries' entire ethos is built on the
assumption that we are flawed, for which they are selling a
solution. And the more successful they are at convincing us that
we are "flawed," the more we will buy their products and the
greater their profits will be.

Naomi Wolf was one of the first women to expose this body
madness during the early 1990s, with her book *The Beauty Myth*.
She argues that the beauty myth gathered strength to keep women
controlled and refocused on their flawed bodies as a backlash to
women gaining economic and political freedom. She believes this

form of mind control gained momentum in response to Betty Friedan's exposure of the "feminine mystique," that exposed the myth and madness behind the smiling, happy domestic housewife. Wolf suggests that:

> *Dieting and thinness began to be female preoccupations when Western women received the vote around 1920; between 1918 and 1925, the rapidity with which the new, linear form replaced the more curvaceous one is startling. In the regressive 1950s, women's natural fullness could be briefly enjoyed once more because their minds were occupied in domestic seclusion. But when women came en masse into male spheres, that pleasure had to be overridden by an urgent social expedient that would make women's bodies into the prisons that their homes no longer were.[20]*

Even though women's bodies have long been treated as needing "fixing," it does seem to be too much of a coincidence that the more powerful we become, the thinner the fashion models become and the louder the message gets about how physically flawed we are: voices that demand us to spend more of our precious time, energy, and money "fixing" ourselves. Time and energy we would otherwise use on empowering and liberating ourselves and demanding equality.

It isn't that we lose control over our youthfulness, our attractiveness, or our thighs, waists, breasts, or hips. What we lose control over is how we feel about our bodies. We lose control over feeling physically strong and trusting our bodies to do what we need them to do. We become deaf to our body's wisdom and knowing what is best for us.

My daughter was the first to show me how much my relationship with my body resembles more of a battle for control than a loving, nurturing, caring, respectful relationship. As far back as I can remember, I have wanted to disown parts or all of my body, wanting it to be different, and starving, threatening, criticising and whipping it into the shape I believed it needed to be in order to be beautiful and importantly, acceptable.

This moment happened in a department store where the six-year-old Olivia and I were hunting for a dress for her to wear to a birthday party. As I stood with her in front of the full-length mirror in the dressing room, I watched her move her body from side to side, admiring her reflection in the mirror as she tried on each dress. She seemed to be assessing if the dress enhanced her beauty without a glimmer of criticism or disgust or that sneer of rejection I see so often on my own face. I was mesmerised by her confidence in looking at herself with such open acceptance. How does she do this? I recall thinking. *How does she accept her reflection so easily, without wanting to change or fix it?*

As I left the department store with a very happy Olivia and her beautiful new dress that swished as she walked, I knew that my young daughter had just shown me a reality I didn't remember knowing. She owned something very precious that I did not. Maybe I lost it somewhere in my past. If I think about it, I do recall small moments during my adolescence and early twenties when I felt beautiful, without any conditions or adjustments. But I also remember that those moments were fleeting, and they inevitably slipped away like sand through my fingers because I didn't know how to hold on to that feeling and make it my own. By then, the voices of body madness had invaded and taken control, created a false truth that had silenced me from knowing that I was okay just the way I am. Just as a virus destroys its host, so do the voices of body madness destroy their host's relationship with herself.

After that first awakening, I started to notice how the conversation of body madness had invaded the women I came in contact with. During a meeting of a women's spirituality group I attended regularly, the discussion turned to how we felt about wearing a swimsuit. I was amazed how unanimous the discomfort about wearing a swimsuit was, regardless of what size we were. We were all women in our thirties and forties and some of us were thin and others larger, but the thin as well as the larger women all admitted to feeling ashamed of their bodies. And it wasn't because we disliked swimming. We all enjoyed being in water, yet more than half of the women in this small group, including one particularly thin woman, admitted that they hadn't worn a swimsuit for years.

I left that discussion group with a bubbling sadness and anger. There is something wrong when women don't feel free and acceptable enough to put on their swimsuit and go for a swim, if that is what they enjoy, whatever age or size they are. I think the "swimsuit discussion" hit me particularly hard because I spent the summers of my youth in a swimsuit at the local swimming pool. I loved swimming, and I was good at it. But now, I don't swim that much. I feel awkward and embarrassed as I walk toward the water and quickly climb in, hoping no one is watching. Too many of us have swallowed whole the voices of body madness without realising the insanity it speaks as it demands we obsessively compare ourselves to the other women in the room, scanning for clues that will ease our fear of being too fat. We don't realise that this conversation is pre-programmed to always make us feel fat, unattractive and unacceptable, because we are guided to focus in on the one woman who is thinner than us, regardless of how thin we are ourselves.

A discussion about body madness isn't complete without mentioning how the medical profession also contributes loudly to the chorus that denies women's right to own and be in control of our bodies. Any treatment of pregnant and birthing mothers as passive and non-participating damages our relationship with our body and inflicts a huge wound at the heart of our female power: our ability to create new life. Sadly, both my pregnancies created a disconnection from my body, as I was expected to hand my body over to the medical team for a safe delivery of my babies. Christiane Northrup says, "Childbirth practices say more about a culture's values and beliefs than any of its other customs."[21] What is missing, says Dr. Northrup, is an understanding that "a mother's emotional and physical well-being is profoundly connected with how safe, supported and encouraged she feels."[22] This, in turn, has a direct effect on her baby's well-being, as well as on her birth experience: "The quality of the mother's outer placenta [how nurtured and supported she is] influences her health as well as her ability to create a healthy environment for her child."[23]

How safe and supported the mother feels also influences her ability to bond with her child and her child's first experiences of safety, nurturing, and love. In her book *Mother-daughter Wisdom,* Northrup calls for women to reclaim our "mother bear instinct,"[24] which has been lost or distorted by a society that is afraid of women's power to create new life.

How different would women's birthing experiences be if we were taught to trust our bodies, connect with them, not see them as dirty or not good enough, and as Tanya of my previous example knew to do, ask for the support we need: the kind of support that keeps the birthing woman at the centre, that listens to her, and encourages her to listen to herself and follow her feelings, needs, and instincts. There was no such conversation at the prenatal classes I attended. The exclusive focus was how to breathe through the pain and take care of the baby. They didn't discuss women's power to give birth, or a women's emotional needs during pregnancy, birth, and postpartum. They didn't mention that emotional process of physically separating from our baby during birth and after breast-feeding. How different would our birthing experiences be if the mother is seen as the all-wise deliverer, and the doctor and medical staff as her supporting team? How different would a mother's place be if her needs were paramount to hospital schedules and doctor's egos?

Imagine a world where women are taught the conversation that befriends our bodies. That same conversation would speak women's nurturing needs without a hint of denial. Eating disorders would be history, and the diet, exercise, cosmetic, and fashion industries would disappear or change radically to become female focused. And women would no longer be invisible.

There are many body madness messages I could talk about, but in the exercise section, I would like to focus on the meaning that our breasts, waists, hips, and thighs have. These parts of our body hold a great deal of power for women, which has been hijacked and used to disconnect us from our body. For each of these parts, I will examine the messages that disconnect us from them, and I will suggest a new, empowering conversation that speaks our bodies' wisdom and self-nurturing as our birthright. I will be changing the focus from "What do I weigh?" to "What nurtures me?" From, "What size do I need to be?" to "What space have I been able to create for myself in my life?" And, "How well do I hide my age?" to "What wisdom have I learned so far?"

Exercises in reclaiming my body's wisdom and nurturing

Our breasts are, as Christiane Northrup says, a "physical metaphor for giving and receiving."[25] They provide a baby with food, love, comfort, and nurturing, and therefore represent the many ways women nurture, love, care for, and feed others. But in a culture that lacks a conversation that focuses on nurturing women, the giving and receiving is out of balance. Women are giving and not receiving nurturing from themselves and others. We live with a set of deep-seated, distorted beliefs around our self-nurturing that make us physically and emotionally ill. Dr. Northrup believes that the message behind the increasing incidence of breast cancer in women is that "much breast cancer is related to our need to be self-contained and self-nurturing."[26] As our mind and body reflect each other's state, our breasts reflect how women are not just physically feeding their babies, but emotionally feeding others without receiving the same emotional feeding in return or feeling entitled to feed themselves. I would add that postnatal depression gives us a huge clue about the lack of nurturing women receive, especially at a time when there is a high demand on our caring and nurturing ability and energy.

The conversation that focuses on our self-nurturing needs is obscured by the overriding conversation that defines our worth by the size and firmness of our breasts. It is time we stop equating the size and firmness of our breasts with our value. Instead, we need to create a self-nurturing conversation that challenges the old voices that accuse us of being selfish and self-centred and asks us moment by moment, day by day, "What do I need to do for myself now?" Ask yourself:

- Do I feel supported by myself and by those around me?
- If not, what do I need to do to start supporting myself and asking for support from others?
- What do I like doing that feeds and nurtures my body and soul?

Our waistline and stomach are the physical manifestation and representation of our inner life force, our intuitive power and self-worth and our emotional and creative space. Stomachs reflect the space we need so we can breathe deeply and take in all we need in life. We breathe to survive physically, but also to speak, and to know our gut feelings and our inner power. When we restrict the space that our waist needs, we also restrict our breathing and with it our gut instinct, our entitlement, and our creative fire in our bellies. Skeletal stomachs and corseted waistlines are silent, empty, and hungry. Tragically, from adolescence onward, we are taught to value a thin waistline over the enjoyment of feeding ourselves.

Our fear that our stomachs are sticking out too much reflects not just our ambivalence with our low self-worth, visibility, and space, but also society's ambivalence and discomfort with visible, equal, liberated women. To redress this, we need to refocus back to ourselves. This starts with becoming aware of how we have internalised the message that women are at their best when we are not greedy or demanding, don't eat too much, and care about others more than themselves. Instead of worrying about how much your stomach sticks out, ask yourself:

- How do I "yes but" myself and stop myself from following my dreams?
- What am I putting up with that isn't sitting well in my stomach?
- What feelings and needs am I stuffing or starving away?

- What lights me up inside and makes me feel alive? Am I doing it?

Our hips hold us up and support our frame. Women do a lot of physical and emotional supporting, mopping up, taking responsibility for and caring for family, friends and others in the community. The daughter and daughter-in-law are often the ones doing the greater share of caring for elderly parents, with little support. Mothers largely take on the primary responsibility for the children. We need metaphorical broad hips to carry all this. Yet, society defines female beauty as having small, narrow hips. The rejection of wide, rounded hips reflects the pervasive fear around voicing women's feelings about whether we're feeling overloaded with responsibility and unsupported.

It is time to claim our need to be supported. Instead of focusing on the width of our hips, we need to focus on creating a strong support base for ourselves, and on setting boundaries and limits on what we can and cannot do. We need to start thinking of what is sustainable, and how we're going to maintain our balance of giving and receiving.

Start asking yourself:

- Am I carrying too much responsibility for others?
- Am I supporting people who are draining me? If so, why?
- What do I need to do to support myself better?
- What help and support do I need to ask for at home and work, and in my relationships?

Our thighs help us move around with speed and strength. They represent a woman's strength to stand her ground and to move forward in her life, helping her to walk toward her goals and run away from danger. Society's fear of women's power hides behind the dictate that thin thighs are beautiful. I once heard a man comment that he was afraid that his girlfriend's rounded, powerful thighs might crush him. Similarly, women's power can awaken great fear of a female takeover bid. This type of fear is a powerful force to resist. It can frighten us into giving away our power and silence us into working on getting thinner thighs.

Claiming our personal power and liberty is not a takeover bid. It is about coming home to ourselves so we no longer feel taken over. Authentic power is about setting good boundaries, about being loving, protective, and nurturing of our bodies, energy, goals and creativity. Instead of worrying if your thighs are too fat, ask yourself:

- What do I need to feel that I am taking better care of myself?
- Do I need others to give me permission to claim what I feel, need and want? If so, why?
- How am I stopping myself from moving forward in my life?
- Am I allowing myself to be treated as less equal?
- Do I believe that my value and worth is related to how thin or attractive I am?
- Am I comfortable with my power as a woman? If not, why not? How does my discomfort manifest itself in how I think and behave?

My prayer is that all women learn to delight in all our curves, the shape of our faces and bodies, and the light that shines from our skin and eyes as being truly magnificent. That no daughter recoils in fear from her mother's aging body or feels that she has to go on a mad diet and exercise regime to fit into her prom dress, party dress, or wedding dress. I pray that mothers and daughters will support each other in their process to give their learned body madness a ceremonial burning. Together, we can challenge and change the images of thinness with which the beauty, fitness, and medical industries bully us. We have that power. All we have to do is begin to question, to speak, and to say no.

Part Three: Being Myself in My Relationships

14: Lessons in Claiming My Voice in My Relationships

My connection with myself should never be sabotaged in my relationships with others. This is because the emotional damage I will inflict on myself will far outweigh any benefits I may get from being in the relationship.

This is true for me, and for every woman reading this book. Yet I have never heard anyone acknowledge that women have relational needs. I have never even heard anyone mention the words *relational needs*. Relational needs seem to be as silent as women's emotional needs. Yet in my work with women, unmet relational needs are a very real and painful struggle. I hear countless women struggling with the age-old female dilemma of: *Do I do what I need, or do I do what others need me to do?* I hear too many react with a shocked "No!" when I ask them if they have told their husband, mother, sister, or friend how they're feeling about their relationship. Many women find it difficult to speak their truth if it hasn't been asked for first. Even though at one level this is a reflection of our lack of entitlement to our own voices, it also speaks a relational truth: If we don't know that our voices are welcome, it makes it excruciatingly difficult to speak.

This insecurity makes speaking shrouded in fear and uncertainty, and has us checking to see if the other person is listening rather than focusing on what it is we want to say. Fiona, a client, described that she felt transparent like a ghost when no one asked her opinion.

Our training for relational silence starts young. I saw my adolescent daughter struggle to keep hold of what she needed to do for herself against the plans she had already made with her friends. She wanted to have a quiet day at home, because she was frazzled by all her recent social activities. But she didn't feel she could change or cancel her plans with her friends. She didn't think they would understand or accept that she needed to do nothing in order to recharge her batteries. I tried to talk to her and show her that her needs were important, more important in fact than her friends' desires, and *that she, too, matters in her relationships*, but she said there wasn't any point in discussing this, because the plans had been set and she had to go.

Relational silence keeps women invisible, blind to our needs, starved, unheard, too responsible, and definitely the proverbial second sex. Relational silence is the problem that has no name, that has always had a name: women's silent relational and emotional needs. Relational silence exposes how our relationships are affected when there is no welcome mat laid out for women to speak. It keeps our relationships a one-way street of caring, and it continues the expectation that women alone are responsible for maintaining and keeping their relationships. Yet, if we keep silent, we will be continuing and colluding with our invisibility. *Silence will only keep us silent.* Silence will not help any of us create relationships in which we are heard, loved, seen and nurtured.

It was with a really good friend, or so I thought, that I started to wake up to my relational blindness. It started with an increasing niggle that I was giving too much. I tried to speak to the friend, but she didn't seem to hear what I was saying. I know that my first attempts to speak were rather uncertain and confused, but I would've expected her to have at least heard my confused and uncertain attempts and responded in a way that meant that she was interested in hearing what I was trying to say. She was, so I thought at the time, a very close friend. Her lack of response was important to not brush away as if I asked for it or deserved it. As my niggle increased and continued to be ignored, I suddenly snapped when she emailed me that she was graduating and wanted me to fly out from England, where I was living, to New Zealand to attend her graduation. She didn't ask if it was convenient, or if I could afford it, or even if I wanted to come. Her assumption that I was totally willing and delighted to jump on a plane encased her words, as if no other reality was possible. For the first time ever, I couldn't find the energy to congratulate her. It wasn't that I wasn't happy for her. I just had no energy with which to say it.

I know this sounds rather mean and uncaring, and it was; I wasn't celebrating her success as I should have and normally would have. But on another level, something powerful was happening that was telling me a far truer picture. For the first time in my life, I started to question not only my relationship with her, but all my other relationships. I started to ask:

"What did she do to celebrate *my* graduations?"
"When was the last time I felt supported and cheered on by her?"
"Why am I feeling so empty toward her?"
"Is this relationship working for me, and what am I getting out of my connection with her?"

The answer I kept hearing was not what my heart wanted to hear. I didn't want to hear the answer "nothing" to every question. Yet, while I loved my friend, I was beginning to love myself more. Being invisible and taken for granted was no longer the mirror I recognised myself in.

As I allowed myself to feel the "nothings," I started to remember moments that I had ignored and switched off because I was starved and needed her friendship too much. One of those moments was how she coldly ignored me when I was crying. At the time I was so shocked by her lack of caring, I stood and walked out of the room to dry my tears alone. Yet I switched it off at the time, and didn't reflect on how her behaviour felt until she invited me to her graduation. I had to become more aware of myself and less emotionally starved before I could cope with the painful truth of how little love, caring and space there was for me in this relationship, and that my love and support weren't being reciprocated.

I tried to talk to her, but she responded in exactly the way I had feared, with anger and silence. Her reaction helped me to acknowledge that I had created a relationship in which I was invisible. Yet my fear of speaking and needing wasn't just a reflection of my own silence. Her reaction when I did speak showed me that my needs were never welcome. This left me little choice but to extract myself from this relationship. I don't feel sad that we have parted. Staying in a relationship in which I feel invisible would've been sad. I am grateful, though, for the lesson she taught me: that in any relationship, whether it's with a partner, parent, child or friend, being invisible is abusive.

Women tell many tales of being hurt in their relationships, tales of having their love ignored, discarded as unimportant, or not returned with the same depth. When women gather, we share and sometimes joke about how hurt we've been. We need to take our hurt seriously if women are ever going to be visible. Today, we are far more aware of the damaging effects of domestic violence. Yet, there is a whole level of relational abuse that remains ignored, because the scars show up on the inside of our souls. They are the scars of being asked to reduce who we are, of having our feelings and needs ignored, and of sacrificing our dreams to keep the relationship or feel loved. *It is an act of soul slaughter when a woman is asked to sacrifice her relationship with herself for the sake of a relationship*. We need to change our relationships from being a victim of silence to claiming the emotional space and autonomy to ask ourselves *What about me, where do I fit into this?*

I invite you to reflect on your relationships, and upon how you have been and continue to silence yourself. Many clients ask me how they can change their relationships when they are only half of the relationship. My answer is that one person definitely has the power to change the relationship. True, we don't have any power over how the other person changes, whether they choose to move toward us or away from us. Remember Andrea, who changed her relationship with her mother for the better, and Jill, whose family didn't like her newfound voice? They both faced this uncertainty. But claiming our voice and relational needs will change our relationships. It will make others see us and take notice of us, and if we stop making ourselves invisible and taking ourselves for granted, they too can no longer play that game.

What's more important is how *we* feel. Feeling strong and entitled can be a hugely powerful antidote against others needing to keep us silent. This strength creates a protective wall around us that others cannot break down or ignore. Use the questions at the end of each chapter to help you create your own conversation that speaks your truth in your relationships. Answering the questions will help you find yourself and stop you from "yes butting" yourself into silence. They will help you discover and speak what you need, when you are hurt, and what you think. They will challenge our collective stoic female past, and support you to become a woman who can support without taking over, without taking it all on, without draining yourself, and without ignoring yourself or using someone else's problems as an easy way of ignoring your own.

15: Claiming My Voice as My Mother's Daughter

It is within the mother-daughter relationship that the signs and consequences of our female emotional starvation are most keenly felt. If a mother is emotionally starved, how will she teach her daughter the language and sense of entitlement to feed herself?

How entitled, free, and autonomous we believe we can be as women is deeply connected with our relationship with our mother, and the legacy of what it means to be female that is passed on from mother to daughter. Mothers teach their daughters the language that speaks our emotional and relational needs, or they teach their daughters the same silence they were taught: how to keep quiet, to think of others first, and to put up and shut up. Evelyn Bassoff, in *Mothering Ourselves*, gives this stark warning. "The daughter of the deprived, self-less woman is not only likely to hold back from living life fully, but in extreme circumstances, she may devote herself to enhancing her mother."[27]

I was born into a female legacy in which nurturing flowed backward for women: back toward the generation before, because each generation lacked knowledge of how to feel entitled to nurture themselves. Nurturing was also a female role in my family.

Daughters were expected to meet their mother's needs, and the mothers were expected to meet the grandmother's needs. When nurturing flows upstream rather than forward from mother to daughter, the result is never good. It will certainly create emotional starvation for all the women.

I don't know how long ago this reverse flow started in my own family, but I do know that my grandmother suppressed her own needs in order to care for her mother, my great-grandmother. I grew up watching Mum feverishly attend to her mother, rushing over to her house whenever she thought she was needed. I never truly understood what the crisis was each time, or why Grandma couldn't sort these things out for herself. But asking that question would've made Mum angry. It was taboo to question my mother's care for Grandma, or to suggest that she could say, "No, I can't today." This would've been an unthinkable act of sacrilege.

And so, being my mother's elder daughter, this was the path I too was expected to follow. I was the next daughter who was to tune my antennae into my mother's needs, and not mind or even recognise that I was suppressing or moulding my own life around my first duty: being my mother's daughter. I wasn't supposed to have any thought or will to be anything but my mother's carer, helper and unfailing supporter, just like Mum and Grandmother had been to their mothers. I was to fill the void that had been created by Mum's disowned and disallowed needs, and to speak the language she couldn't speak for herself. This meant that I was never to say no to her. I was to always think of her needs and be her emotional helpmate, the one from which she drew strength and validation. Most of all, I was never to abandon her physically and emotionally, just as Grandma and Great-grandmother never left their mothers or each other.

Care-taking can often have a rather controlling side effect to it. I was also expected to want what my mother wanted, to think what she thought, and to never question her decision or judgement. Caring for and being just like your mother is seen in my family as a mark of the greatest respect and honour that a daughter can bestow on her mother. Being a dutiful daughter proves to her and everyone else that she is a good mother, because she has a good and grateful daughter. And if I slipped up and dared to voice a thought or need of my own, the punishment was harsh. I would find myself rejected and ignored because I had been selfish and uncaring.

During my pre-teen years, I learned to agree with and apologise for anything and everything. It was my survival strategy. I would say sorry and swallow my anger at the injustice of it all. Being "in with Mum" was critical for my well-being, because being "out" was too harsh on my developing sense of self-worth. It is hard to hold on to your own sense of right and wrong when it is only in the process of being formed and the "normal" in your family makes you bad when you aren't following the rules set out for you as a dutiful, compliant, agreeable daughter. With silent treatment and a heavily disapproving atmosphere as punishment for stepping away from being a dutiful daughter, I learned to think that I alone was responsible for keeping people happy with me— and that upsetting people would not only be my fault, but also could mean the end of the relationship. Mum had somehow learned to use relationships as a weapon of control and punishment. She passed on her own disconnection from herself as she taught me to disconnect from myself: to fog up, to not dream, and instead to focus on her, mould my life around her needs, and above all, don't shine too brightly, because in our relationship intimacy meant loss of self.

These relational rules meant that even before I was born, my relationship with her was doomed to be a battleground, a battle that started to rumble from about twelve years of age as my need to become my own person rose up to fight for my survival. Something very healthy and instinctual kicked in during adolescence that saved my life. An unmistakable voice made me know that my relationship with my mother was a battle to the death. At the time I didn't understand what the warning was all about, but I knew with great certainty that I was going to survive.

I have now learned to understand the truth my instinct was speaking way back then. It was warning me that I was in a relationship in which my emotional survival was at risk. The rules of our relationship dictated that a daughter has to emotionally die to herself so her mother can use her daughter's life to create the life she couldn't have and didn't know how to create for herself. These were ancient rules, and exceedingly destructive rules. My instinct was warning me that if I tried to sacrifice myself for my mother's emotional well-being, I wasn't going to survive emotionally myself. It was an either-or choice, and from that young age, I knew with cold-blooded certainty, without any guilt or regret, that it was going to be I who survived. I wasn't going to die to myself so Mum could live.

As it turned out, I was right not to have worried about Mum's survival, because when she eventually realised I wasn't going to be the daughter she wanted and needed, she turned first to my brother, and then to my sister to get her needs met.

Even though my instinct gave me that vital push to claim my own life, that was only the beginning of my battle. I had to come to terms with and heal my normal need to be mothered; my emotional starvation that made me need her even more; and the poisoning of my self-worth through the name-calling, anger, criticism and silent rejection. For years, I wondered if Mum's criticism that I was "selfish," "bossy," and "too prickly to be loved" was true. But as I started to heal, I recognised that these names didn't reflect me. They reflected Mum's own fears about herself, and because she didn't know how to deal with them, she passed them on.

It's hard to form a good feeling about yourself when the mirror your mother holds up is cracked by her own broken sense of self-worth, an attitude she herself inherited from her mother. You need to find enough emotional distance and muscle to recognise the pattern of inherited low self-worth. It's impossible to have that degree of objectivity when you are severely emotionally malnourished. When you're starving for normal motherly affection and attention, you frantically search for a magical cure to heal your mother so she can see you and show you she loves you. In my young woman's mind, I created a fantasy that if

I looked hard enough, I would find this one word or one thing that would make Mum love me. My starvation also made me yo-yo in and out of favour with Mum for years. Whenever the distance between us felt too much, or when I felt too bad about myself, or too starved, or in need of a mother's presence, I would go back to Mum, swallow my feelings, and do whatever it took to get her to talk to me again. Now, I know there is no such magical word or action that will change her behaviour. I also know that yo-yoing in and out only leaves me feeling more starved and hurt. I didn't, and don't have the power to change or heal my mother. All I can do is heal and change myself.

Healing myself wasn't easy when my mother's silent treatment was treated as normal and never questioned in the family. This created a strange sort of reality, the kind in which you know you haven't done anything wrong, but you're still being punished. It is an upside-down kind of reality, where even though you cannot think what you have done to upset her, you're still bad, and still responsible for having upset her.

It is important to remember that though my family's dynamics may have been extreme, they are far from unique. Teaching females that femininity is synonymous with caring only for other people's feelings is the same upside-down reality where our feelings don't exist, only someone else's.

I arrived into adulthood not knowing how to speak in my relationships. I doubted myself most of the time, I didn't know I could assert myself when I did know what I wanted, and I didn't know that boundaries existed and that I had some of my own. After I left home, got married and had my children, my relationship with Mum got progressively worse. It seemed as if the more independent I became, the more she withdrew into her angry silence and the less she wanted to know about me. I recognise this now with the benefit of hindsight, but back then, Mum's behaviour was completely baffling and felt like a stab in the heart.

During my twenties I became depressed. Having ingested too much criticism and angry silence, I believed I deserved to be ignored. I was also drowning in caring for my young family. Not owning any boundaries, needs, or voice, and not having examined the legacy of selfless caring I had grown up with, I was mindlessly repeating the selfless, dutiful caring I had so disliked in my mother and other women. The same selfless caring I had vowed not to repeat.

During the worst days of my depression, Mum made a rare visit that had a miraculous effect of injecting the clarity I desperately needed to help me see through the fog that was obscuring my vision. I had just returned from visiting my sister, where I had broken down and cried, admitting for the first time to her and myself that I had no clue who I was. My sister had obviously reported this to Mum, because soon after arriving home, Mum unexpectedly knocked on my front door. After I opened the door she marched in, sat down, and proceeded to give me a lecture about how I was giving my children too much freedom, which was obviously the cause of my unhappiness. My children were five and two years old at the time. After she finished saying what she had come to tell me, she got up and left.

As I watched her leave, I was at first confused and speechless. And then I understood. For the first time, I understood that she didn't *want* to know. She hadn't asked me how I was, or what was wrong, or if I needed any help, because she didn't want to know the answer. She didn't want to know that our mother-daughter script wasn't working for me and that I had lost myself in trying to be her dutiful daughter. Knowing that would've meant acknowledging the same truth about her relationship with her mother. And she certainly didn't want to know that my depression was in any way due to her distance and anger. Knowing and understanding me as her daughter would mean knowing and understanding that she, too, had lost herself in trying to be her mum's good and loving daughter, and that her fevered care-taking of her mother had created and colluded with their respective disowned responsibility for themselves and their relationship. This was all too much to know and change, so she simply didn't want to know it.

Seeing Mum leave that day helped me to take one step toward placing the responsibility for her behaviour back with her. It was a moment when some of the poison that had eaten away at my soul evaporated, a moment where distance started to be created as I saw my first glimpse that maybe Mum's anger wasn't my fault at all. Mum, in a strange way, gave me a gift that day. She gave me the beginnings of a clarity that helped me rewrite my "dutiful daughter script" in a way that was to release me from trying to be the daughter she needs me to be. Now, I could rewrite that script into a script that gave me the entitlement and strength to set up and enforce my own boundaries, whether she liked it or not, and whether she respected them or not. I started to realise that my emotional and physical well-being, if not survival, depended on establishing my boundaries with her to give me more control over my life.

There were other wake-up calls that jolted me forward on my journey to create a new normal that was centred on my connection with myself. One of those jolts was writing a letter to my parents. It was time I came out of hiding. I needed to challenge my fear of their reaction to hearing my truth. I wrote a letter because I didn't think I could find the words to say what I wanted to say in person. I needed time to think and reflect and choose my words carefully. In the letter, I tried to explain what my relationship with them felt like and what I needed so we could connect better. Sadly, my words were met with a deep, angry silence, and my letter was never mentioned. I heard from my siblings that Mum paraded my letter around the family to gather support against me.

Even though I didn't get the response I needed and hoped for, I am still glad I wrote the letter. I needed to do it for me, to speak anyway, regardless of how they may or may not have reacted. I needed to claim my voice even if it wasn't welcomed, and to see the bald, sad, painful truth of how I was being treated.

Two other incidents stand out as landmarks to my recovery. The first one occurred after my grandfather died and his sexually abusive behaviour was finally admitted within the family. I had long wondered, and maybe hoped, that this was the reason why

Mum never wanted Grandma and Granddad to baby-sit us when we were children. As she shared with me the long-held secret, I asked her if this was why she didn't want him baby-sitting: if this was why she was so upset after the only evening my grandparents ever baby-sat us.

Mum replied with a half-laugh, saying "Oh no, it had nothing to do with that." She went on to explain that, as a mother, she believed that she had to take care of us, and during that evening when Dad and she had gone out, there was an earthquake. She had been angry with herself for not being there, just in case something happened.

I couldn't believe what I was hearing. All this time, I had felt some sense of comfort and safety with Mum, because I had assumed that she was trying to protect us from our grandfather. Suddenly, my assumption was proved wrong. What I heard in her half-laugh was that she had made that sacrifice for herself: because of her own beliefs about what motherhood required of her, rather than what I or my siblings might have needed. I felt dead cold as I quickly ended our conversation. In that moment, I took another big step in emotional separation. I knew that Mum didn't get it, that she didn't understand her need to protect not just her own life, but also the lives and experiences of her daughters. I knew that Mum's view of "okay" didn't come close to matching mine, and there was no point in me even trying to explain. I had come face to face with the thick wall of denial that lay around my family that protects one or a few from being responsible for their behaviours, and that sacrifices the rest of us to their need for control and power. Her response left me feeling completely unprotected in my relationship with her. My rights had no voice because daughters were okay to be sacrificed. All I could do was walk away, because I knew that surviving in this type of environment is impossible.

The second incident occurred a few days before my father's funeral. Mum had made no effort to inform me that Dad was dying, yet I instinctively knew I couldn't afford to speak my anger, because I needed to attend his funeral. I think I switched off my feelings in order to be able to say good-bye to Dad. I was standing with Mum in her bedroom, looking out at Dad's beloved garden, when she said that one of the last things Dad said to her was that us kids would've ended up in the gutter and not made anything of ourselves if it wasn't for Mum. As her words sunk in, I turned around and walked out of the room and out of her house.

I didn't respond. I knew there was no point. Though I could imagine Dad saying this, I also knew that he was proud of me, of all of his children. I knew he didn't mean those words in the way Mum said it, and I knew what she meant. *Yet whatever I achieve, whatever I do, however brightly I shine,* I thought, *she cannot give me any credit for it unless she is given full credit for my achievements. And I must not achieve too much. My achievements must be making her feel unhappy about the things she didn't get to do.*

As I walked away, I severed the final emotional strings that were keeping me tied to needing her approval. I had finally seen the truth that I would never get her approval, at least without great sacrifice to myself, and that hoping for it was only keeping me down and emotionally dependent on her. I had to set myself free so that my daughter was free. The legacy of mother-daughter emotional dependency and enmeshment Mum had inherited and passed on to me had to end with me. I had to be the last unmothered daughter in my family.

Since then, I have stumbled about in my journey, not always knowing my way, until suddenly I would wake up and realise I had ignored something deeply hurtful, often for years, because I had switched myself off. The truth is, it is much harder to express old anger that didn't get expressed at the time the hurt or offence was inflicted. Today, I am glad to say that I am no longer angry, just sad. Too much silence has killed my love for Mum. In its place, I just feel sadness. I feel sad that my mother and I didn't get the mothers we needed. I am sad that Mum didn't get enough understanding from Dad. I am sad that Granddad never had to account for his behaviour. I am sad that Mum lived during a generation when the mould for mothering was suffocatingly tight. Even though Mum is fully responsible for her behaviour, I also believe she didn't have the power to change or stop the inherited emotional starvation and disconnection from being passed on. She is a product of her generation, upbringing, and life experiences. She was too much of an unmothered daughter and inherited too much of a dead zone to mother me.

I feel a strange kind of peaceful calm in knowing she did the best she could, and that it's now my turn to do what's best and right for me. I have come to a place where I hold sadness, peace and tragedy all together when I think of her. It is tragic that her fear of losing me led her to suffocate me, which made her fear a self-fulfilling prophecy. She lost me because she couldn't let me breathe.

If we are desperately trying to be loved by someone who is unable to love us, the only thing any of us can do is turn around and walk away. While I was desperately knocking on Mum's door, hoping and pleading for her to let me in and feel loved by her, I didn't notice that the doorknob was missing on my side of the door. Mum was the only one with a doorknob, and the only one who had the power to open the door to let me in. And while I was frantically knocking, I didn't see the people and opportunities that could love me. I was so focused on being loved by her, I lost touch with my own power, strength, goodness and instinct. All any of us can do in those relationships is to turn around and walk away, leave them responsible for their relationship with you, and claim your own ability to believe in your worth and ability to feed yourself.

Mother-Daughter Relationship Checklist

Here is a checklist I use with my clients to help them assess how healthy their mother-daughter relationship is. I use these questions at the start and end of our time in counselling to check how much has changed for them to that point. The aim is to be able to say yes, all of the time or most of the time, to each of these statements:

1. I can say what I feel without feeling guilty.
2. My privacy is respected by my mother/daughter.
3. I am free to make my own decisions and mistakes.
4. I can be honest.
5. I feel encouraged and supported to grow and change as my own person.
6. Our relationship has changed to incorporate my own growth and change.
7. When we disagree, my opinions and feelings are heard and respected.
8. I feel heard and loved by my mother/daughter.
9. I enjoy my mother's/daughter's company.
10. I feel happy with who I am.
11. I have my own friends and support network for advice and companionship.
12. I make my own decisions about what rules and boundaries I want to live by.
13. I feel that my rules and boundaries are respected.
14. I take responsibility for my own needs and choices.
15. I am healing my own painful and wounding experiences.

16: Claiming My Voice as My Father's Daughter

I can still see Dad and Mum at the kitchen sink as they were spring-cleaning the kitchen cupboards when Dad turned to me and said, "One day you too will get a husband who will help you with the spring cleaning." I remember thinking *Great, why does he only have to* help? Yet, for the first ten years of married life, I did all the cleaning and never questioned that it wasn't all my responsibility. I don't recall even asking for help. *Why?* I asked myself. *Why did I do it all? Why did Mum say nothing that day?*

Fathers have a huge influence in teaching daughters what attention and understanding they can expect in their relationships, and especially from men. How they treat their daughter's mother and their partner or wife teaches the daughter whether she can expect to be heard and loved. Fathers communicate a woman's place in the home, whether his partner or wife is his equal or the family servant. And if the father is the only one working outside the home, they have an important part to play in teaching their daughters about the outside world and the world of work. He will teach her how it feels to be paid for one's skills and time, and how to negotiate and expect to be heard, rewarded and respected at work.

I grew up watching my father becoming more and more distant, retreating into his garden, his books, and his own world. I watched him change from being a rather dapper man who was extremely proud of his appearance to someone who didn't care very much about his cleanliness or clothes. It felt to me that the less he cared about his appearance, the more distant and disinterested he became in me. I also watched him change in his behaviour toward Mum. During the years when his appearance mattered, he seemed to delight in showing Mum attention. I remember how pleased she was with a beautiful long brown faux-fur coat he had bought her. But the scruffier he became, the less attention he paid Mum, until he completely tuned her out when he bought a huge set of radio headphones and walked around with them all day on his head as if they were permanently glued to his ears. He literally tuned Mum out.

My journey to reclaiming my voice needed to include how my Dad's gradual withdrawal affected me. As a young girl, I loved helping him in his garden. Spending time with him while he planted and collecting horse manure from the paddock behind our house were wonderful days. It was during my adolescence and adult years that silence invaded our relationship. He died just four short hours before I landed home, in New Zealand, having flown from England in the hope of seeing him one last time. So it was alone that I had to face my fear of being unimportant and easily discarded by a father I adored. I never got to tell Dad how his lack of effort to keep in touch felt. But I also know that if I had told him, my words would've made no difference to his behaviour. He didn't change for Mum. He didn't change for anyone.

My relationship with my father deeply influenced and formed my sense of entitlement in my relationships. He too taught me that my needs had no voice. That I wasn't to ask or expect anything. And if I dared to request some attention, I was to be happy with whatever little or nothing he could give. Not having experienced anything different, I assumed this was normal. I took on all the responsibility for the emotional work of keeping in touch. This helped me create a façade that stopped me from wondering too loudly why Dad and others weren't putting in the same level of effort, or any effort at all. Without understanding that good relationships have a giving and receiving flow to them, I shut myself down to protect myself from feeling bad and unimportant and soothed myself with any crumbs of attention and love, even though deep inside Dad's lack of interest and effort hurt.

Dad also greatly influenced my relationship with Mum. It was no secret that Mum and Dad had agreed in their marriage that Mum would be in charge of everything inside the home: looking after the home, the children, and I guess, facilitating how the family members get on with each other. Dad was in charge of the outside: the garden, growing vegetables and earning money. I knew early on that Dad wasn't the person to go to with questions about homework, friends, or life in general. He helped me paint my first home, and pruned my trees and supplied vegetable plants. His stock answer to "inside questions" was "That is Mother's department, go and ask her." When I telephoned to inform them that I had broken my foot, Dad, who answered the telephone, said, "That's Mum's department" as he handed the phone over to her. As if by magic, he vanished out of the picture without asking me how I was, or how it had happened, or God forbid, if I needed any help. Dad just carried on with his daily routine as if nothing was amiss.

Birthdays and Christmas were an inside job, so Mum's department. But when Dad came home on my sixteenth birthday with a bag of cherries for me, my starved heart filled with joy and amazement that he had thought of me and remembered it was my birthday. Just like the little match girl in the Hans Christian Anderson story, who in her frozen alone state imagined a beautifully decorated Christmas tree and a table laden with food in the light of her matches, I too was prone to such hallucinations. In this single bag of cherries, I imagined I saw the proof my heart was yearning to know: that I was important and special to my father. Sadly, Dad never did something special like that again. Yet, in my starved heart, I have stretched those cherries out to last a lifetime of believing, despite the silence, that I must have been important to him.

But really, how do we know if we are important to someone if they don't show it in their actions? The last evening I spent with Dad was nearly six years before he died. We went to have dinner at their house the night before we flew back to America, where we were living at the time. Dad was having treatment for cancer and his prognosis was uncertain. After we finished eating, Dad got up from the table and announced he was spending the evening playing cards with his friends because it was his regular card evening. I remember feeling a shock go through my body as he said this. I actually felt detached from my surroundings, as if I was floating near the ceiling above everyone and watching my family interact like a movie that you aren't actually in. I watched him walk out the door excited about the evening, without a word of good-bye or a mention that I was flying back home the next day. No one, including me, said how hurtful and just not okay it was for him to go like that and not spend this last evening with me. If I had been in his shoes, whether I was sick or not, I would've gladly forfeited one card evening to spend with my daughter. I would've grabbed all the time I could to be with her. That evening, none of us knew this was the last evening we would spend together.

I flew home having switched myself off with a "Yes but Dad loves to play cards." And around my heart I built my protective wall even higher, walling off my uncertainty that I could need, lean on, be important to and expect others to do their work to connect with me. I didn't see the red flags of invisibility when Dad didn't ask me anything about me. He didn't ask how I was, what I was doing, or how my life was in America. No one around that dinner table asked me about my life, in fact. It was as if I wasn't actually there. But what was I to do? I wanted to keep contact with Dad. I needed him. I needed to rescue someone I could create a fantasy around for my lighted match, when it all became too cold. I had to have one good parent. One parent who I thought loved me. After all, he once gave me a bag of cherries. And in my fantasy, I continued to breathe in the thick air of denial that hung around my family: air that let Dad off the hook for everything.

Dad died blaming Mum for his lack of connection with me, and so did I for many years. Our last telephone conversation ended with me asking him if it was too hard for him to have me visit with Mum present. He answered "Yes," and with that, I silenced my need to see him one last time. I switched off my anger about his lack of contact because we both wanted to believe that "If it weren't for Mum, Dad would've made more contact." Blaming Mum was the story with which he left me long before he died.

After Dad died, the story of blaming Mum started to crumble in my mind. I started to see how it worked for Dad to collude with Mum's jealousy. We both blamed Mum, because we both needed to let Dad off the hook. He needed it because it absolved his responsibility, and I, because I needed a loving parent. I think Dad liked it that Mum was in charge of the cooking and cleaning and childcare, because that meant he was also taken care of. On more that one occasion, he said he married Mum because he knew she would be a good mother for his children. Mum seemed to take this as a huge compliment, but to me it was an insult. What I heard him say was that he saw Mum as a baby-making, house-cleaning, nose-wiping, homework-helping, PTA-attending machine. To me, he treated Mum as only a mother, not a partner, companion, woman, person and individual in her own right. But as a young woman I didn't blame Dad for his sexism, I blamed Mum. It was somehow more her fault for accepting his stereotype of her. I was angry with her for not standing up for herself, and not giving both of us a voice for our freedom of choice, individuality and sense of partnership with our husbands and partners. Dad's sexism eroded my relationship with Mum and reduced my respect for her.

I even think Dad created some of the conflict between Mum and I. It suited Dad if Mum was angry and resentful at me, because whilst Mum was busy focusing her anger on what I wasn't doing, she wasn't noticing what she wasn't getting from him. It suited my "peace at any cost" father. It isn't a very nice thing to think, but I believe Dad willingly sacrificed his relationship with me so his life was sweet with Mum. He was willing to let me take all the heat and deflect it away from him: heat I received in the form of jealousy when I got the crumbs of attention she was also starving to receive from Dad. Dad's lack of attention to both of us set Mum and me in competition with each other for any crumbs of attention he might have bestowed on any of us.

The task both Mum and Dad had set for Mum to do was doomed from the start. It was an impossible task for Mum to be the total carer for our large family, with only Dad's financial support and vegetables from his garden. I remember Mum grumbling sometimes that she was the one who got all the criticism if something went wrong. And she was right. It is too much to expect the mother to be everything to her children. She needed a lot more than money and vegetables from Dad. We all did. We needed Dad's nurturing and a real sense of his love and devotion. We needed Dad to nurture Mum and to claim his part in the emotional nurturing of our family. The inside/outside split meant that the balance of caring was extremely off. It left Mum taking care of Dad, but Dad not taking care of Mum, which created an emotional wasteland for her, a wasteland that made her competitive and jealous of any love and care Dad might have shown. It also meant that her children, and especially I, her daughter, were expected to meet the emotional needs her husband wasn't meeting.

My relationship with Dad, my parents' relationship with each other, and our family as a whole didn't function well with this inside/outside split of male and female roles. It denied Mum the entitlement to fulfil her need to have a life outside of the home, and it denied Dad's need to express his nurturing side. Dad was an uncharacteristically emotional man for his generation, but he was taught from boyhood that emotions and nurturing were not male jobs. Relationships and fatherhood were only about providing money.

The great lesson Dad taught me is that there is no peace at any cost, because this type of peace comes at an incalculably high cost. He passed on a legacy of silence that is highly destructive. Keeping quiet or even silently enabling a conflict between other people to deflect the heat away from yourself is greatly damaging for everyone. Keeping your head down or trying to sneak your life around someone else, as I saw Dad do when he secretly went swimming or visited people, is not an honest way to live.

Even though Dad will always be responsible for his behaviour, it is now my responsibility to heal my fear that I'm not worth connecting with, and to learn to know in my heart that Dad's lack of interest and connection never did speak my own worth. Rather, it speaks Dad's inability to connect, his history, and his disowned wounds. I am worth caring about and connecting with regardless of Dad's behaviour. And even though Dad was terrible at connecting, I do have a few memories in which I am in no doubt that he did love me. These moments are different from my starved matchstick-girl fantasies. I feel him around me since he died; he came to me hours after he died, standing in front of me, smiling, before he turned around and walked into a bright white light. This vision happened twice while I was in a plane flying out to see him and unaware that he had died. I am in no doubt he appeared so he could say good-bye before he left this earth.

Exercises to claim and speak my needs to my father

Ask yourself in any relationship:

1. What feelings am I ignoring or not speaking in order to keep the peace?
2. Why do I feel I have to keep quiet?
3. What makes me afraid of speaking?
   What do I fear will happen if I speak?
4. What is keeping quiet doing to me physically and emotionally?
5. What support do I need to get to help me speak anyway?

Next, how did your relationship with your father influence your relationship with your mother? These questions are relevant even if your parents are divorced or deceased.

1. How did your mother feel about her relationship with your father?
   Did she feel loved and supported by him?
2. How did your mother react to you when you had contact with your father?
3. How do you feel about your mother's reaction to you?

Have you and your mother ever discussed your respective relationships with your father? (This discussion is only appropriate between adult daughters and mothers.)

In your relationship with your father:

1. Can I say what I need from him?
2. If not, why not?
   What is stopping me?
   Is it something within me, or my father, or both?
3. What needs do I have that I haven't received or asked for?
4. How well do I know my father?
5. What parts of his history do I need to know about?

If your relationship is unhappy or distant, ask yourself: "What do I need to do to make it better for myself?" If change isn't possible, ask yourself: "What do I need to do within myself in order to be at peace with how it is or was?"

If your father is emotionally unavailable, have you internalised his distance as saying something about your worth?

17: Claiming My Voice as a Mother

Women will not enjoy full equality and visibility until they wake up and realise how damaging female sacrifice and selflessness is to everyone: women, mothers, daughters, sisters, and yes fathers, sons, and husbands too. When enough women start waking up and realising the damage, the world will witness a burning-up of the concepts of female sacrifice and selflessness, on a scale never before witnessed.

Yet until this collective inferno occurs, women will continue drowning in a sea made up of the needs and wants of others. The closest I came to drowning was one morning weeks after my daughter was born. John had gone back to work after two weeks off, leaving me at home, alone, with our nearly one-month-old baby daughter who didn't sleep day or night and our lively three-year-old who needed a lot of entertaining and asthma medication four times a day. I was also in charge of the mountains of washing and the daily cooking and cleaning. That morning, I decided to strap my fretful baby into her front pack so I could hang out the washing. As I bent over to pick up the laundry basket, she suddenly started to flip over in the pack. I dropped the laundry basket and grabbed her just before she ended up hanging upside down.

Shaking, I looked at her to see if she was okay. She seemed fine, oblivious to what had just occurred. But I wasn't fine. What remained of my already depleted confidence and frayed nerves lay shattered on the ground as I sank to the floor, shaking and sobbing. I couldn't bear to think of what might have happened, of what I might have been responsible for. I couldn't think how it happened, except the only explanation my exhausted, fried mind could come up with, *I'm not safe to be with the kids*, and *I clearly am not the capable mother everyone thinks I am and expects me to be*.

I didn't tell anyone about what happened that morning. I eventually got up, hung out the washing and kept going, hiding my shame because I knew no one would understand. I had already learned that the only conversation people want to hear is how joyful and blissful mothering is. Admitting that I was fed up with the daily grind of cooking and cleaning, wiping noses and bottoms, or that I was yearning for a break, or for something else to enliven my mind, wouldn't be received well. I would be met with a horrified look, followed by a sharp intake of breath and the usual accusation "Oh you don't mean that, surely you love your children!" Older women would empathise with me, but not with the energy of really listening and encouraging me to challenge my status quo. Their empathy would focus more on patching me up to keep me going. My grandma's warning echoed all around me, saying, "This is a mother's lot to bear and we are to bear it gladly." Admitting I need something outside my child's needs was a serious offence as a mother. As a mother of two, my needs had no language, no legitimacy, and no value. My needs were taboo because meeting my children's needs was all I was allowed to want.

Now, as I look back at myself, a young new mother, alone, crumpled and sobbing on the floor, responsible for two small children, I feel angry. I was invisible, taken for granted, and a neglected young woman and mother surrounded by blind neglect from my family and a society that denies the conversation, "Who is taking care of Mum?" It makes me sad to remember how acutely blind I was to my situation. I had learned to believe that neglect was normal and okay and that my grandma's words formed the limits of my entitlement.

On the floor that morning, I was a hollow woman who had been launched into motherhood with silence, and then silenced into mothering my children from a place of emotional emptiness. I was expected (and expecting myself) to mother without the understanding that in order to mother, I needed to be mothered and nurtured myself, and that the well from which my mothering flowed needed daily replenishing. I was expected to give and give and care and care without being registered on the family's hierarchy of needs. I was expected to continue the mothering mould that my mother, grandmother, and millions of mothers before me and around me had been poured into: a mould many of these women never found a way to break, remould or change. A mould of mothering that sentences women to mother and survive from a place of emotional starvation.

My story isn't unique. Mothers everywhere have their own stories of neglect, starvation and silence. I hear these stories every day, including the emotional consequences to mothers and their daughters when a mother is expected to mother from empty. I hear how the mother's emptiness affects her relationship with her daughter, and how she can pass it on to her daughter. I see mothers who are so emotionally hungry, they can only see their daughter as a source of feeding, even elderly mothers who demand and expect their adult daughter to meet their needs with little thanks and understanding that her daughter has a right to her own life and time. These mothers are trying to be fed through a kind of "payback" from their daughter for all the sacrifice and giving they have done. Yet, in trying to get fed through their daughters, these mothers don't realise they are passing on their emotional hunger to their daughters. When emotional feeding is turned into an either/or situation, either the mother or the daughter, feeding becomes shrouded with ambivalence and guilt, which leaves a daughter confused and often unable to emotionally feed herself and replenish the well from which she gives, just like her mother.

I hear of angry, near-to-death-starved mothers who emotionally beat their daughters up with powerful guilt-tripping statements and years of well-practised martyrdom because they haven't learned how to be emotionally responsible for themselves. They treat their daughter as if she is somehow responsible for, or the cause of, her emptiness, with statements like, "Oh, I thought you were dead" when she hasn't called on time. Or, "You do it, you're so much better at it than me," when the mother doesn't want to take responsibility for something. The emotional blackmail is unspoken, but clearly communicated: *"Do it exactly the way I want it done or you clearly don't care about me."*

A common problem for this generation of mothers and daughters is emotionally distant mothers who are unable to celebrate their daughters' success. As daughters embark on territories that their mothers could only have dreamt about, these mothers are suffering from feeling jealous and mourning their lost dreams: dreams that were said to be inconsistent with being a female and mother. Ashamed of their jealousy, in the hope they will never be discovered, these mothers hide their understandable feelings of loss and thwarted dreams behind a cold exterior. But their daughters know something is upsetting Mum, that something is wrong, but because she doesn't know what, the daughter is left wondering if it is she. She instinctively feels that her success is upsetting her mum, so she too starts to hide herself away.

I know all too well how confusing it is to understand what is behind a mother's coldness and distance, and how easy it is to think I must be to blame. But we are not. Maternal jealousy is a result of maternal starvation and being expected to mother in a too-restricted mould. This creates a web of envy, jealousy and martyrdom, an inability to take care of yourself, an expectation to be taken care of and a lack of freedom to claim your own life. This web will continue unchallenged and unchanged if we don't start asking, "Who is taking care of Mum?" and, "What do I need?"

I hear mums who are in the process of losing themselves in their mothering as they say with desperation and shame in their voices that if they don't get a decent amount of time for themselves very soon, they are in danger of running away. Mothers who have had enough, who are at the end of their rope and can no longer cope with all the demands and juggling of their time. Mothers who are way beyond exhausted, and who are at that place that has no word for being on the floor, can't do it anymore, all given-out exhausted. These are desperate, anxious mothers who don't know how much is enough, what is good enough, what the boundaries are that are protective of their time, sense of self and energy, and how to say no. These are both stay-at-home mums and working-outside-the-home mums. All sorts of mums are frantically responding to everyone else's needs, juggling an impossible list of demands, never feeling they are doing justice to anything, and feeling guilty and uncertain as to whether they can respond to their own needs, *if* they are still able to hear them at all. Tragically, these are the same mums who are at the early stages of becoming an emotionally starved "payback mum."

It terrifies me to realise that on the day I sat crumpled and sobbing on the floor, I was on the path of becoming any one of these emotionally starved, distant, overloaded and controlling mothers. I was mothering in an environment that had no nutrients to help me develop my own sense of self-nurturing and identity as a woman first, who is also a mother. So how did I change my course and recover my voice and sight from being so acutely blind? How did I eventually start asking, "Where were the five other adults (that morning) who were equally responsible for this new member of the family, as well as my welfare? Where were John, my parents, and parents-in-law? How did I discover what I feel, need and want, and how did

I learn to nurture myself in a family and society that pays mere lip service to maternal needs and even shamelessly twists around maternal needs to mean neglecting our children?"

The first eye-opening change I made was an internal one. I dared to believe that motherhood is not a career! As a psychotherapist, I hear every day of the damage inflicted on mothers, their daughters and sons, and the mother-daughter relationship, when motherhood is treated as all defining of a woman's identity and her only career. This turns motherhood into a gilded cage that is painted with blissful scenes of mothers smiling, laughing, saying, "Oh, isn't being a mother just wonderful" while denying any voices that don't fit with this Madonna image of selfless sacrifice. This cage turns motherhood into an either/or conversation: either a mother's needs or our child's needs.

My mum and grandma were all-mothers. I witnessed them, and many other all-mothers, slowly disappear from view. It made my relationship with my own all-mother more difficult. I found it hard to relate to Mum as a woman, because the only part she showed me was her being a mother. I also felt great pressure to be the "right" sort of daughter who showed her and the rest of the family and community that she was successful at mothering. It felt as if I had to get Mum's grades, and show that her sacrifice and effort were successful and worth it by how I behaved and how well I did, and by the choices I made.

I didn't want that for myself or for my children. I didn't want my children to feel they were my "project," one for which I wanted to achieve an excellent grade. I wanted my children and me to be free to find our own success on our own terms. I didn't want my sense of success tied in with what my children chose to do with their lives. I also needed to stop the legacy of jealous mothers who couldn't bear to see their daughter follow their own dreams. I didn't want to be jealous of my daughter because I had missed my heart's yearnings.

Motherhood needs a paradigm overhaul. It needs to be pared down to its bedrock, without the layers of silence and either/or conversations that trap mothers into only being able to make a choice between meeting their child's needs or their own. We need to forcefully reject the conversations that blame and shame mothers for neglecting their child's needs if they dare choose to meet their own. Motherhood is, at its core, a relationship in which we nurture our child's journey of discovering who they are. It is about creating a loving, nurturing relationship with our child that feeds and nurtures *them* and values *both* our needs. It is about creating a definition of motherhood in which mothers matter, are not servants, and are off-duty sometimes.

I began with claiming a few hours each week to study part-time for a university degree. For the first years, I was happy with a few hours each week. But gradually, the longer it took to complete my degree, seven years in total, the more resentful I became of squeezing my already-part-time study around everyone else in the family. I was also becoming resentful of always being in charge, while John "helped out," baby-sat, and took the kids on fun outings to the park to give me a break. Even when he was in charge, I still packed the diapers and food and made sure he had everything. I still did a lot of the thinking and holding of it all in my head, which was exhausting. It made my head full of things to do with little room to think about me. Little room to let go and have fun! Naomi Wolf describes that giving instructions made her feel like a general and not too good about herself. She said it made her feel "that I am bossy, a control freak. But more than anything, it makes me feel responsible for everything. That feels burdensome. Lonely. Pulled in fifteen different directions."[28]

As my eyes started to open to the inequality, career damage, invisibility, being taken for granted, responsibility overload, and toxic guilt I had agreed to from before I became pregnant, I started to see that for fathers it was different. I wanted a piece of their kind of "different." I too wanted the time, freedom, and most importantly, the continued sense of still being myself, a woman, even though I am also a mother, that John was still allowed. He was allowed to be a male, a person, even though he was a father.

My mother-in-law helped me to see the difference between fathering and mothering, between John and me. She said, "I don't know how you do it all, how you study and look after your kids."

At first I responded with a defensive, "I do it just like John does, he works and has children too." But as I mulled over her words, I recognised that it was very different for John. John didn't need to squeeze his career and work around his children's needs, because I did ninety-five percent of the childcare and one-hundred-percent of the cooking and cleaning. I remembered how my mother-in-law stopped bringing meals around as soon as John went back to work, after Olivia was born. I had never questioned this before. I hadn't noticed what that said about how she saw me: what she thought my duty and role was. Through my work with women, I now see this with completely new eyes, how this is a form of unacceptable abandonment of new mothers, which is directly linked to and a contributing cause for postnatal depression, anxiety disorders, and low self-worth.

"What about your children?" and "What about John's doctoral studies?" were the first comments I received when I announced I was embarking on postgraduate study. Ignored was the fact that John too was a full-time student. Clearly it was different for John and I, as father and husband, mother and wife. For mothers, our dreams are to be second place to our role as child-carer and husband supporter. No one asked John how he was going to take care of his children and study at the same time. The clear message: He was free to fully engage in his studies, whilst I was not.

It wasn't easy to grow my sense of being a woman—a person first—when each time you admit to being a new mother, or at home with young children, you are committing social suicide. Over and over again, this admission would mean the end of the conversation, except for how the kids are doing. Suddenly, I had nothing interesting to enquire after or to contribute. Andrea Buchanan describes her experience of this in *Mother Shock* in the chapter *The Invisible Woman*.

*I meet someone at a business lunch and at the mere
mention of my twenty-month-old daughter the
conversation quickly dies. Over and over I am greeted
as if I am a normal, interesting person, and then once it
becomes evident that I am a mother, I immediately
become less appealing, more easily dismissed.*[29]

It is hard to keep hold of the whole self when all around you parts
of you get blocked off, not enquired after, not valued, as if they no
longer exist or are important. I have never heard John complain
that people stopped asking him about his work, or his football,
after they found out that he has kids.

You cannot help but walk away from these encounters bruised.
But I also walked away determined to not let their limitations seep
in and limit me. I could not let the shameful guilt-tripping of
mothers, the one that twists taking care of ourselves into a sign of
lack of devotion or neglect of our children, limit me. We have to
remind ourselves that at the heart of motherhood is a powerful
lioness who will do anything to care for and protect her young.
And does a lioness neglect herself? I am sure, though I know I am
mind-reading a lioness here, she knows that if she doesn't take
care of herself, she won't be able to care for her young.

The new paradigm for mothering must include the concept that
to mother, we need to be mothered ourselves. This means
answering the questions, "Am I taking care of myself? Am I being
the kind of mother I need for myself?" Mothering is more than
just taking care of our children. It is also about mothering
ourselves and feeling entitled to do whatever it takes to feel
emotionally well fed and nurtured. To ask ourselves, "Who is
taking care of me?" whether the question is welcome or not,
answered or not, or turned around as evidence of our lack as
a mother. This question is not a sign of a neglectful mother.
Rather, it is a sign of a healthy, whole, nurtured, giving-from-a-
replenished-well mother.

Recently, I had a magical few hours with my daughter that
showed me I've not only been able to stop the passing-on of

maternal jealousy, but also turned the tide of emotional starvation. Olivia and I had spent the afternoon searching for her prom dress. I felt honoured to be able to share this milestone with her, and to share in how beautiful she looked in all the dresses, especially in the one she selected. As I reflected on our lovely day, I realised I'd come a long way. I felt sad knowing that my mother will never experience the joy of watching me find a dress for a special occasion. She will never experience this because I will not share an opportunity like this with her. She doesn't know how to give me a moment to say what I like, or allow my preference to be the best for me. I know from experience that if I attempt to share good moments in my life with her, I will end up feeling invisible and unheard, and horrible about our time together. It is a bittersweet feeling of success, but I have spent too many years on the bitter side. Today, I celebrate the "sweet" I've been able to find.

Exercises in claiming myself as a mother

The new conversations about mothering that nurtures us and doesn't limit a mother's identity, options or loyalty must:

- *Stop the stay-at-home versus working-mother argument.*
At a conference on mothering,[30] I witnessed mothers react to a speaker who was describing her inner reaction to sitting and reading in Borders bookstore while pushing her child in the pram to keep the child asleep. She said that, at a glance, she looked like a stay-at-home mum sitting in a bookstore. She reacted with some anger, because she wanted everyone to know that she was actually an academic doing research. Some of the women listening reacted with "What is wrong with being a stay-at-home mum?" Her need for people to know she also had another job was heard as putting down stay-at-home mums.

I didn't hear her put down stay-at-home mothers. I heard her say her feelings in an "and conversation" that spoke both her needs and her child's. I heard her react to the low value of being a mother. I heard her desperately trying to have value by wanting people to know she was also in paid employment, because we all know paid employment is valued so much more than unpaid mothering. And I also heard her react to how, as a mother, her academic job was invisible, as Andrea Buchanan bemoaned earlier. I also heard her say that she wants to be seen as a whole woman who does many things well, often at the same time.

It's time to stop the conversation that tears down mothers who stay at home and mothers who work for money. We need to stop the either/or conversation that keeps mothers' needs off the hierarchy of needs. Either/or is divisive and destructive for all mothers; it pits us up against each other, using up valuable energy and obscuring the real issues of rights, equality, liberty and support for all mothers, whether at home or at work. It creates a situation where the oppressed are tearing at each other rather than challenging the silent discrimination and confinement that creates the conversation in the first place.

- *Crack wide open the illusion that mothers have access to a full range of choices.*

Choice is a myth that patriarchy beats mothers up with to make us feel guilty and submit to our unsupported, undervalued status. Our economic situation and level of family and community support affect our choices. Our level of education and qualifications affect our choices. Being a woman affects our choices. Our child's needs affect our choices. The lack of flexibility and sexism within the corporate world affects our choices, as Kate Reddy, a fictional London banker, discovered in *I Don't Know How She Does It* by Allison Pearson.[31] No longer able to juggle mothering and her corporate job that expected nothing less than complete devotion, Kate quits, because opting for the part-time "mummy track" is the same as committing career suicide. Her husband thrives with their lifestyle change. She doesn't. She is left looking longingly at the foreign exchange figures while she waits in line at the bank.

Also, staying at home or working outside the home is not always a choice. Mothers work because we need to: We value our economic independence, and for many it is an emotional necessity, because we aren't at our best at home full-time. I went to university and then worked because I don't feel good about myself being financially dependent and at home full-time. It doesn't work for me. During the years my children were small my choices were limited, because my first child wasn't the type of child who thrived in childcare. He needed someone close to him to look after him. This meant I had to rely on his father or grandparents to take care of him when I attended university classes. Unfortunately, I didn't have a family that recognised my dilemma. All they saw was that my first and only job was to take care for him, while they tolerated my studies in small doses as "something on the side." And because my lioness heart felt my son's needs more strongly than my own, I reduced my needs to accommodate him. All I could achieve, to honour my child's needs and my own within my limited childcare resources, was a few hours a week.

- *Create a conversation that helps mothers emotionally prepare for motherhood.*

Mothers need to talk through how we adjust to being pregnant and how we rearrange our sense of freedom and knowing of ourselves to include this new person. Parenting books rarely mention anything about a mother's emotional adjustment and nurturing needs. (The only exception I have found is Christiane Northrup's book *Mother-Daughter Wisdom.*) As I have said, we are launched into motherhood with silence. I searched on *www.askDrSears.com,* the in-vogue parenting advice manual, and found nothing on emotional adjustment or maternal needs. The topic didn't exist. I did, however, find something that Dr. Sears calls *The Shutdown Syndrome.* He warns that a baby can emotionally shut down if its needs are not adequately responded to.[32] This is true. But is this not also true of mothers?

Mothers thrive if nurtured and don't thrive if not nurtured. Where is the chapter on "Mother Shutdown Syndrome" that warns against mothers shutting down emotionally when their needs are not heard and responded to? Warning that mothers who aren't nurtured end up fantasising about running away? That they end up crumpled on the floor in a heap of exhausted confusion? That they end up with depression or an anxiety disorder or in grave danger of becoming a demanding payback grandmother who, after a lifetime of nurturing everyone, is fed up and craving the attention she has long needed but never got?

It seems so obvious to me, it leaves me speechless that this conversation isn't part of our normal dialogue. Its silencing makes me angry. I am angry at the unrecognised harm being unleashed on mothers every time their needs are suppressed, ignored, treated as selfish, treated as threatening their ability to nurture their baby, or seen as unfeminine. And I am also angry because silencing this conversation gives a very clear message that a mother's needs are of no importance. But as Tanya said, "It is amazing what women can do when we are supported." (See chapter 10 "Claiming My Visibility and Value") She knew something that many parenting experts and others, who devalue and silence a mother's needs, are still very ignorant about. To begin the conversation, ask yourself:

1. How do I feel about myself as a mother?
   List the areas you feel good about and not good about.
2. In the areas I don't feel good about, what do I need to do differently to change how I feel?
3. What messages did I receive from my parents, parents-in-law, friends, media, and parenting books that are making me feel inadequate?
4. What do I need to do to make me feel more adequate?
5. Is there anything else I would like to be doing at the moment?
6. What do I need to do, or believe, that will help facilitate this?
7. What support am I not getting that I need?
8. What images or statements make me feel judged as a mother?

9. What mantra can I start saying to myself that will protect me from being affected by mother-blaming?
   For example: "I am a lioness for my children's and my own needs."
10. What limits and boundaries do I need to put in place so I don't end up exhausted and feeling used?
11. How much time for myself do I have? Is it enough?
12. What do I need to do to secure enough time for myself on a daily/weekly basis so I can recharge my energy levels?

18: Claiming My Voice as My Daughter's Mother

It is within the mother-daughter relationship that our silent female scream can be heard and healed, or silenced and inherited. The mother-daughter relationship is central to the empowerment of women. When we empower mothers and daughters, we empower the world and the generations to come. – RH

The notion that girls aren't as valuable as boys showed its torturing face even before my beautiful, shining daughter was born. I was twelve weeks' pregnant and having a routine scan performed by a doctor who had thin, straight, yellow-white hair, a large fleshy face, and a bow tie. I distinctly remember the bow tie because I remember thinking how silly it looked. Whilst lying prostrate on the bed with my stomach bare and my bladder full to a worrying degree, the bow-tied doctor asked me if this was my first pregnancy. I replied that this was my second. "Oh," he said. "What is your first child?"

"A boy," I replied.

"Oh well," he responded with relief in his voice, "then it doesn't matter what this one is."

I was stunned. I literally didn't know what to say. Reactions reeled through my mind, but I couldn't find anything to say. Lying exposed on the table didn't make me feel empowered to say anything angry. I'm not sure what my partner heard, because John, too, said nothing.

As I walked out of the clinic, I debated whether I should make a formal complaint. I didn't, but now I wish I had. I needed to have said something to push the sexism in his words back to him. Speaking would've got it off my chest and not left me carrying the awful feeling that girls are still less wanted. I needed to say something for my not-yet-born daughter, for all the women who were once unborn girls who, in his statement, were only welcome if a brother had preceded them. And I needed to say that this kind of sexism is harmful, demeaning and insulting. I needed to voice my feelings, because I left feeling that my silence communicated that what he said was okay. That maybe I even agreed with him. How else would this bow-tied doctor learn to hear anything different if I, if we all, kept silent?

Olivia was absolutely wanted. Giving birth to Olivia was the most profound life-giving and lifesaving moment for both of us. I believe that the vision I had moments after she was born saved both of our lives. It was a powerful vision that shook me awake and held the key to exposing and changing our mother-daughter legacy. As I heard the midwife say that I had a daughter, a chill ran through my body and a voice in my head said, *"If I don't get my shit straight, this new girl isn't going to have a happy life."* It was a strange voice—half my own and half someone else's. I heard it clearly, as if it needed to say its message loudly enough for me to take notice. And its warning was very clear. My new daughter wasn't going to be happy if I didn't get my relationship with myself and my mother sorted out.

As the words sunk in, the hospital room faded into blackness and I saw and felt my own, and my female ancestors', shared experiences of abandonment, abuse, and lack of being mothered, and our resulting sense of selflessness and emotional starvation. I saw it like a timeline drawn out on the dark wall, with the events and experiences that had created dead zones in the women who had come before me. I saw how each mother had treated her daughter in the same way she had been treated by her mother, which then meant she passed on her sense of selflessness and emotional starvation onto her daughter, creating generation after generation of unmothered daughters.

I could feel how dark and damaging this thread of emotional starvation was for my female family. Not knowing how to feed your starvation had created a hard, bitter jealousy toward a daughter's ability to be fed and receive love, and her youthful beauty and opportunities. And the daughters, sensing their mothers' unhappiness, became afraid of losing their mothers' love and so rejected any feeding opportunities that might upset their mothers. I saw how my grandmother and mother had clung to their emotionally unavailable mothers and spent their lives caring for them as if their mother was the only life raft they had to hold onto. I felt how deeply afraid they were of losing their mothers, and how they had each paid too high a price for giving into this fear.

At the end of the timeline, I felt the crushing weight of expectation that I too should not abandon my mother. I remembered hearing Mum say that she made many of her choices based on what would be easier for her mother. And now I was expected to do the same. Was this also my new daughter's future? My vision warned me of the dangers of dead zones and silenced dreams. It warned me of the cycle of how emotionally disconnected, starved, and manipulative mothers create emotionally disconnected, starved, and unmothered daughters, who in turn become manipulative mothers themselves. I was the last emotionally disconnected, starved, and unmothered daughter. Was I going to become the next manipulative mother to this tiny new daughter? Was she destined to be the next emotionally disconnected, starved, and unmothered daughter?

I could feel the suffocating pain that would tie my daughter to me and me to her. I felt the enormous weight of responsibility of Mum's denied and disowned voices and life, and how my daughter would end up feeling mine if I didn't claim my voices and life. I saw how I was silent to myself and far too focused on what Mum and others needed from me. I knew I could easily hand this on to my daughter, just as it had been handed to me. But I also knew what it would be like for her. She would grow up feeling unheard, unloved, undervalued and rejected for her uniqueness, just as I had. At only minutes old, Olivia had already helped me see that I had only one choice to make. I had to look forward and save myself in order to save her.

As this surreal experience faded and I regained my awareness of the bed beneath me, John standing beside me, and the room we were in, I knew with unwavering certainty that this legacy had to stop, and stopping it had to start with me. So with the birth of my daughter, my mission to understand and learn about the ties that bind mothers and daughters began: a mission to understand what happens in the silent undercurrents between mothers and daughters, and what can either empower or disempower, connect or disconnect, separate or enmesh, heal or harm. Understanding mothers and daughters is lifesaving work. Lifesaving not only for Olivia and me, but also for every woman. This understanding saves our female energy, because *who we are and how we feel about being a woman is deeply connected to our mother. It is within our relationship with our mother that we begin to learn about ourselves as a woman. And it is within the mother-daughter relationship that we have the power to change our lives and world to include our female voices.*

Mum's silence increased after Olivia was born. She visited me in hospital, but all I remember was Dad sitting with me, and Mum wandering the corridors with my sister's daughter. The next time Mum made contact, or it may have been when I broke the silence, Olivia was six weeks old. I wonder if the arrival of a granddaughter also alerted Mum that something was wrong between us. But because she didn't know the conversation that spoke her feelings, all she knew to do was to speak through her silence.

I felt acutely alone and weighed down with responsibility during Olivia's early years. I keenly felt the emptiness behind me where I needed my mother to be, and the enormity of the task of changing the flow from the past, a task I didn't yet fully understand or know how to achieve. With all this, it wasn't a surprise that I suffered from postnatal depression. My condition wasn't recognised at the time, and it took me two years to find my way through it. I know this because I remember the day when I suddenly felt an unfamiliar joy creep into my heart that I had a daughter. Olivia was two years old, and together we went out to buy something girlie for her. We bought her a pair of red rabbit hair clips.

It is hard to admit that it took me two years to celebrate having a daughter, but being harsh on myself doesn't tell my story; instead, it would ignore the lack of nutrients that celebrate our shared femaleness in my female heritage and environment, and in my relationship with my mother. I couldn't celebrate Olivia's femaleness because I hadn't learned to celebrate my own. At that time, the picture of femaleness I saw reflected back to me was that females take care of everyone, are wrong for wanting anything, and are sad most of the time.

An issue about clothes stands out for me as one of my first lessons in how important it is to own my own needs so that I don't confuse Olivia's voice with my own. Olivia was three and demanding to have a full say in what she wore. Dressing had become a battle. She loved to wear dresses, regardless of the weather or where we were going. At first I fought with her over it, and tried to get her to dress appropriately. But then one day I woke up to why this issue bothered me so much. I hadn't been telling the whole truth through my argument that Olivia needed to dress for the weather. A large part of it had nothing to do with the weather or with her. Seeing Olivia looking beautiful and pretty made me feel frumpy and unattractive. I had lost my enjoyment in looking good myself, and during my depression had stopped taking care of my appearance. All my three-year-old Olivia did was remind me of what was missing for me.

Seeing this dissolved the "battle of dressing" between us. I refocused my energy on dressing myself and let her find her own way with her clothing choices. I am grateful I woke up early. This battle held the potential of passing on my own bad body-feelings. My spoken and unspoken reactions to her could've easily taught her to wonder if there was something wrong in enjoying dressing herself, feeling beautiful, and getting attention for looking beautiful merely because it upset her mum. History would've repeated itself. Again.

Mothering my daughter, learning to listen to her fledgling voices, and discovering how our relationship affects us both, is a life-giving journey. It is hard to witness her being influenced by the same voices of silence that silenced me. It can leave me feeling powerless. But as her mother, I am far from powerless. I can teach her the questions and voices of entitlement that are powerful antidotes to her socialisation for "silent niceness." I can keep asking her "What do you want?" and "How did it feel when you didn't do what you needed?" I can hold the questions and entitlement for her until she is ready to take them on herself. Holding up the mirror of self-focus for her will help her to eventually learn to make the connection that when she doesn't listen to herself, things don't go well, and she ends up not feeling too good about herself.

Though this may sound simple, it isn't always easy to untangle the threads between us. "Niceness" lurks behind many corners, like an unseen guest that creates conflict and pressure in relationships. It can take some effort to discover its underlying presence. An example of this was when I became increasingly irritated and feeling put-upon when Olivia asked me to go around picking up her friends when they had organised an outing. Reluctantly, I did it. Sometimes I would say that I was feeling put-upon, but more often than not, I would swallow my irritation because I was confused about whether I was being unreasonable. Olivia's reaction to my occasional no would also serve to reinforce my confusion.

Eventually, Olivia and I sat down and really talked about how we were feeling. What she said helped me to understand my reaction. She said that she felt pressure to be nice to everyone, and if I said no to helping her be "nice," she would feel anxious and afraid that her friends would think she wasn't being nice. Her honesty made our exchange so much clearer. I could see that because she didn't know how to handle her anxiety, and because she didn't understand her "disease to please," she turned it back on me and said that the problem was my unwillingness to help.

She wanted me to collude with her lack of boundaries and help her avoid anxiety. For my part, sensing her anxiety and not understanding it pushed against my fear that I was being a selfish, unsupportive mother. Both our "diseases to please" were knocking against our wobbliness to say no.

Mothers and daughters are emotionally very connected. Even if nothing is said, daughters will pick up when Mum isn't right, and mums know when their daughters are troubled or upset. Emotions, if not owned, can also be passed between mothers and daughters, which Karen and Abigail, a mum and her fifteen-year-old daughter who came to see me together, illustrate.

Karen was going through a painful time with her husband, Abigail's father. She had discovered that he had been having an affair for the last three years, and she was struggling to deal with her anger and hurt. Abigail had been an easy child until about six months before, about the same time Karen found out about the affair. Over the last six months, Abigail had become increasingly difficult to handle. She was misbehaving, rude, and generally bad tempered. Over the weeks the three of us talked, it became clearer that Abigail was reacting to her mother's anger and hurt and her own confused loyalty toward both her parents. Abigail loved her mother and hated seeing her mother hurt by her father. But she also loved her father. Feelings were not being talked about in the family, and especially not by Karen and her husband. I have seen many daughters acting out their mother's unacknowledged and unspoken feelings, as if they are their own. Karen needed to start focusing more on herself and healing her relationship with herself and her relationship with her husband, rather than focusing on her daughter's behaviour as a way of avoiding herself.

I wish all mothers and daughters a great deal of honest sharing as we grow as girls and women and co-create a world that no longer sees or treats us as only nurturers, mothers, objects, and the unequal sex: a world that embraces the many, varied voices that describe our own and collective descriptions of femininity.

Exercises in claiming my connection with my daughter

If we are to ever fully understand our relationship with our daughters and heal the epidemic of mother-daughter conflict and misunderstanding, we have to change the themes that harm this vital relationship. As mothers, we have to dare to be honest with ourselves and not shy away from some uncomfortable truths. This is courageous work, which I always feel in awe of every time a mother comes to me with the hope of improving her relationship with her daughter. All these mothers are pioneers!

Following are areas that mothers need to reflect on in order to become conscious about themselves as mothers and to provide an antidote to the voices of female silence for their daughters.

- *Beware of a defensive reaction against saying anything negative about mothering.*

The numerous ways that mothers are blamed for anything and everything, and the resulting fear this creates about not being a good enough mother, can create a defensiveness against really understanding the undercurrents between mothers and daughters. Being defensive can be just as silencing as mother-blaming. Being defensive silences the healthy and necessary examination of what harms mothers and daughters. If we are to claim our power as mothers, and the power of the mother-daughter relationship, we have to understand the dynamics between mothers and daughters, and importantly, the themes that harm and heal this relationship.

- *The denial of a mother's needs is the biggest threat to mothers and daughters today.*

The level of conflict between a mother and daughter is a direct reflection or barometer of the level of emotional disconnection suffered within the mother and daughter individually. On a more aggregate scale, the degree of mother-daughter conflict within a community reflects the degree of emotional disconnection amongst women. The epidemic of emotional disconnection amongst women is creating a corresponding epidemic of mother-daughter conflict, estrangement, and misunderstanding.

Emotional disconnection and starvation is the biggest threat to mothers and daughters today. It harms a mother's ability to hear her daughter's voices and it harms a mother's ability to teach her daughter the language that speaks her emotional needs. Mothers who don't speak that language for themselves cannot pass it on to their daughters. Instead, they are in danger of passing on their own disallowed needs. Change this threat, and the relational problems of manipulation, misunderstanding, toxic guilt and guilt-ridden loyalty will no longer be an issue.

- *Mother-daughter conflict is a mirror reflection of women's place and inequality within the family and society.*

I see many mothers who feel deeply hurt that their adolescent daughters are openly saying that they don't want to be like their mothers. In part, this may only be a daughter voicing, in a clumsy way, her attempts to separate and become her own person. But sometimes these daughters are saying a truth that needs to be heard. I have found it interesting that in most of these cases, the mother is feeling unhappy and unfulfilled herself. As I talk with these mothers, I help them see that their daughters aren't saying they don't love them. All they are doing is pointing out that they're sending their daughters an inconsistent message. On the one hand, they are encouraging their daughters to do well at school and dream of what they want to be. But through their own disempowerment, they are showing their daughters that working hard at school and expecting to create your own life doesn't become a reality. They are showing them that women end up stressed out and unhappy, and taking caring of everyone. It makes sense that daughters are reacting to this message and saying they don't want to end up unhappy and running after everyone, just like their mothers do.

The conflict between mothers and adolescent daughters, in particular, is a mirror reflection of what happens between mothers and daughters when they are trying to connect in a society that teaches women to be silent and to switch off their voices, needs and dreams. During adolescence, girls react against being switched off in favour of being nice and acceptable. Focusing on just individual mothers and adolescent daughters is useless. To understand why there is this theme, we need to understand the themes of female silencing. We need to start seeing adolescent conflict as a healthy cry against something that isn't healthy. Looking at the visibility of the women in the family and society will go a long way to understanding a daughter's cries. To awaken a healing dialogue, we need to look past their dress, their offensive and destructive behaviour and their music, and reflect on the anger they are communicating in order to understand what they are saying.

- *Daughters need to feel heard and understood by their mothers in order to feel loved.*

The formula is: Being Heard + Being Understood = Feeling Loved.

This is the reason why the silence around a mother's emotional needs is so destructive. Mothers need to be in touch with their emotional needs before they can hear their daughters and respond. Hearing and understanding doesn't mean that the daughter needs her mother to agree with her. It means that the daughter needs to know her mother understands what her daughter is thinking, feeling, and desiring. It makes sense that daughters need this from their mothers, because feeling heard and understood creates the foundation of feeling fully known by others, the very thing that female silence erases.

- *Being our own person needs to be the new normal.*

Mothers and daughters need to create a new normal in which mutual empowerment creates the weft and warp of their relationship. This means that both are encouraged to be their own person and all they can be. It means that, as a mother, I am a "good-enough" mentor who doesn't get it right all the time, but that doesn't mean I have to beat myself up with guilt when I get it wrong. It means that my daughter isn't responsible to make up for what I don't feel entitled to do for myself. It means building a relationship in which both of our needs and feelings matter.

This new normal smashes the female myth that "being our own person means being alone." The more connected we are to ourselves, the more able we are to connect with others. The limitations we have in taking care of and understanding ourselves will create the same limitations of understanding and relating to our mother or daughter. Being our own person is not dangerous to connection, it actually enhances it.

A healthy Mother-Daughter Relationship includes:

1. Conducting honest communication.
   Feeling heard and understood by each other.
2. Taking responsibility for your own needs, feelings and dreams.
3. Living the life you desire.
4. Having your own network of friends.
5. Having awareness of, and respect for, individual and generational differences and similarities.
6. Respecting each other's privacy.
7. Being able to say no to each other.
8. Expecting that men and women are treated as equals.
9. Understanding your shared female legacy.
10. Openly rejecting negative stereotypes and expectations.

19: Claiming My Voice as My Son's Mother

*A son could wonder endlessly why his mother did
not intervene when he needed her or why she expected
him to cope by himself. Men do not realise that
women believe the legends about masculinity.*
Babette Smith, *Mothers & Sons*[33]

Since the moment I saw the beautiful, not-yet-fully-awake face of
my precious son Ben, I knew that keeping him connected to his
emotions was going to be a battle. A battle I didn't yet fully
understand then. Having grown up with a father who I saw cry
when he was upset, I already knew that crying doesn't threaten a
man's masculinity, as the prevailing cultural message would like us
to believe. I also knew that macho "action-men" role models and
violent video games teach boys that being male means that you
fight and win through being physically powerful. They model a
masculinity that is about having power over other men, and
definitely over women.

When Ben was a baby, I was generally left alone to soothe and
cuddle him as much as he needed. But as he turned four and
entered preschool, the battle for his emotions gained momentum.
The first warning that I was "doing it wrong," even damaging him,
came from the other mothers at a playgroup. The mothers (no
fathers attended this playgroup) would look at me with obvious
disapproval when I didn't encourage Ben to go out and play on his
own when he wanted me to stay with him while he was playing.

They didn't say anything directly, but their looks and comments clearly communicated that my lack of encouraging Ben to go out and conquer the playground on his own was extremely remiss, even negligent of my son's "apparent" developmental needs. I tried to ignore their looks, but it wasn't easy to prevent their disapproval from eating away at my mother's instinct that was telling me that right now, Ben needed me close.

Only a few years later, when I turned up to the same playgroup with my independent-spirited daughter who enjoyed nothing better than to go out and conquer, I saw more clearly how my son's emotional needs had been treated as not-okay for a young male. This time, they again frowned because, now, I wasn't encouraging my daughter to remain close. The socialisation of gender stereotypes and the pressurising of mothers to teach their children to fit into the right-tight box start very early. And the lessons are very clear. Boys are to be taught to be independent and not need anyone; girls are to remain close. I, though, had children who needed the exact reverse.

Next came school. Ben, like many boys, wasn't ready. He could've done with another year at home, but he was five and in New Zealand, five-year-olds start school. Every time I tried to talk to his teacher about how he was coping, or if I lingered a little too long, his teacher would sharply tell me, "He is fine." But this didn't reassure or convince me. I persisted with my questions until finally the teacher, with unveiled exasperation in her voice, said, "Too much coddling isn't good for a boy. Leave him alone, he is fine."

I knew that he was struggling, and that I wasn't going to get support from his school. I decided to follow my own instinct and kept him home from time to time, with the excuse of illness, which gave him the breaks he needed to ease into school life during that first year.

Close on the heels of being told off by my son's teacher, came my mother-in-law's warning not to turn my son into a "mummy's boy," because that would greatly harm his future social acceptability. I cannot remember what sparked her to say this, but I remember how confused it made me feel. She had raised two sons, so a part of me wondered if she was passing on some valuable piece of wisdom, mother to mother. Looking back, I think that was exactly what she thought she was doing. But as I was to discover, the truth that she spoke, that "mummy's boys" get slaughtered in the playground, is only a small part of the wisdom. Ben and I needed wisdom on how to navigate a male culture that dictates that emotions make men weak and not fully male, without losing his connections to his emotions and our emotional knowing of each other.

Ignoring looks or comments by relative strangers is one thing. Even the schoolteacher is only important for the year your son is in her class. But being warned that my listening to and responding to my son's emotional needs was turning him into an unacceptable "sissy" or "wuss," which could ruin his future social life, packed a punch. Like any mother, I wanted the best for my son. I wanted to give him all I could, to help him grow up happy. Threatening any mother that her nurturing and instinctive choices are harming her child kicks us right at the core of our mother love. It makes us wobbly, afraid of ourselves, and it tunes our antennae away from our inner knowing.

It wasn't until my son was nineteen that I was shaken awake to how powerfully that punch had influenced me. The incident that awoke me occurred when my sixteen-year-old daughter was about to fly to New Zealand alone, and her father and I wanted her to fly as an unaccompanied minor. Both Ben and Olivia reacted to this. Their reactions showed us how differently John and I had treated Ben, when he flew to New Zealand alone, at sixteen, only a few years earlier. It had never occurred to either of us that Ben might have needed support. We just assumed that he would be okay going alone, just as we assumed Olivia would not be okay. The wider family also reinforced this sexism. No one once suggested that Ben should fly as an unaccompanied minor, but with Olivia, they all wanted to make sure that she was going to be "looked after."

It was a huge shock to realise how unaware I had been. I had completely ignored Ben's emotional needs, even though I had resolved to do so when he was born. How had this happened? How had my resolve been eroded away, especially since I had witnessed young men talk about how they felt unwanted and let-go-of as *they* neared the end of their adolescence? I heard male student teachers share how they felt abandoned, cast-out and forgotten after they graduated because many of their families didn't expect them to come home. During the years I supervised student teachers, I noticed a distinct difference between the family expectations of female and male students. With only a rare exception, the female students were expected to return home after graduation and find jobs in their local schools. The male students however, were without exception free to find jobs anywhere in the country or world. Both struggled with these expectations. The female students felt caged by their limited freedom; the male students felt cast adrift, as if they were expected to make it alone without help.

Sixteen years after hearing my mother-bear instinct tell me that I had to battle to keep my son connected to his emotions, I too had set him adrift without even realising what I was doing. I think two interconnecting forces blinded me to my son's emotional needs, slowly, but severely. Firstly, I was blinded with fear by the threat that if I remained emotionally in tune with Ben I was in danger of harming him. No mother wants to knowingly harm her son. Secondly, my gaping ignorance about how the male culture was moulding my son and moulding how I felt about myself as his mother, and how it was influencing our relationship, made me vulnerable to believing the cultural voices and unaware of my blindness. I didn't realise how I had been manipulated by fear to back off so the male culture had a free hand in shaping my son into an "acceptable" male.

Even though I had spent years studying women's silence and the mother-daughter relationship, I hadn't questioned loud enough the silencing that the male culture inflicts on its boys and men. In Babette Smith's words, I was "bamboozled by patriarchal mysticism."

*Women have complied [with the moulding of boys]
"enthusiastically and sadly" for centuries. If they were
unhappy with the effect of masculine induction on their
sons, they accepted that it was their judgement which
was impaired, not the cultural yardstick. With
insufficient power to either object or change an
entrenched tradition, their usual response to the
impassable "mystery" of masculinity has been to
abrogate understanding. In modern terms this is usually
expressed by reactions which range from a despairing
"don't know what gets into them," to an admiring
"boys will be boys."*[34]

I hadn't understood that men are just as much victims of
patriarchy as women. In the conversation that blames men for
keeping hold of the reins and for not wanting to power-share, I
hadn't seen that, below the surface, men are socialised into
valuing physical strength and being unemotional, competitive,
and not needing anyone. In my blindness, I hadn't seen that the
definition of masculinity that society holds firm doesn't
necessarily tell the truth about how men really are deep inside. To
keep the illusion of male dominance and supremacy alive, males,
too, are boxed into a mould that speaks its own *Silent Male
Scream*: a scream that tells the story of how boys are taught to
silence all their emotions, except anger, until a dead zone forms
around their emotions, turning them into hollow, angry,
distrustful, emotionally illiterate, emotionally hungry males.

I wish I had read Dan Kindlon and Michael Thompson's book
Raising Cain years earlier. In it, they say they believe that "boys,
beginning at a young age, are systematically steered away from
their emotional lives toward silence, solitude, and distrust."[35] My
mother-in-law's warning and the disapproving looks from the
other mothers were all part of the cultural conversation that
moulds masculinity into being separate and different to what is
defined as female. I had only been looking at the surface, and
didn't realise how much my father's comment that "girls are much

more difficult to bring up" (Read chapter 3 "Taught to Be Silent") was another cultural mask to hide the intense complications in the male culture that ripple undetected, way below the surface.

I had also not thought beyond being angry with Dad, John, Granddad, and other men for not responding to their wives', sons', and daughters' emotional needs. I hadn't made the connection that maybe many men can no longer respond emotionally, not unlike how, after years of emotional disconnection and silence, women can become so dead to themselves they can no longer connect with their own and someone else's feelings.

In my fear-driven ignorance, I had inadvertently colluded with the emotional silencing of Ben. I had allowed him to grunt, change the subject whenever it became too emotionally intense, and silence me with a flash of anger. I let him brood on his own in a way I would never allow or expect Olivia to. I have always expected her to talk out her feelings, but somehow I had believed the male culture's teaching that a mother needs to respect her son's "apparent" need to go into his cave and sort it out on his own. I had let Ben slip away between the cracks, essentially handing him over to a culture that is threatened by femininity and emotions, a culture that will train him to become silent, emotionally illiterate, and emotionally hungry, while giving him only anger as a way to voice his feelings and emotional needs.

But when I see Ben do his share of cleaning the house, read his heart-warming letters, feel him pat me on the back, and hear him ask how Olivia is, I know I must have kept some of my promise to him. I see him still in touch with his emotions, empathy, and nurturing, because when he is inquiring after Olivia, he isn't asking so much about what she's doing. He wants to know how she is *emotionally*.

Ben has also taught me a lot about reinforcing my boundaries and not feeling that I have to "please" my friends to be liked. I think boys are way ahead of girls on how to set boundaries. I will never forget the moment I overheard Ben say to his friend, "No, I am busy, I cannot come over right now." With that, he put the telephone down and walked past me on his way back to the computer to continue his homework, muttering half to me and half to himself, "I am not going to waste my time if my friend is bored. His boredom is his problem, not mine."

The strength of clarity in his voice slapped me in the face. I was amazed how clearly he knew that he had a right to his own time. Ben woke me up by showing me something I didn't, but needed to own.

Mothering Ben has taught me to understand how he has to juggle two sets of diametrically opposed emotional rules: our home standards that value emotional honesty, and the male culture that demands complete emotional denial. If I listen carefully, I hear him verbalise this struggle when he tells me with a half-joke that I am turning him into a "poof" when I encourage him to say what he is feeling. For years, I missed hearing how he was saying, through this comment, that he was afraid and confused about how to show his emotions in a culture that doesn't accept boys being emotional.

I think I have also misinterpreted Ben's need to have time away from his friends. I was right in understanding that his need for time alone or to be with the family was, in part, because of who he is. But there was maybe another reason. Maybe he needed time out from the pressures of being a certain type of male. The "killer instinct" pressure to compete and win in the male sports culture and the constant one-upmanship can be exhausting and overwhelming, and it certainly damages men's self-esteem.

As Ben, John and I sat watching a football player being sent off for bad behaviour during a televised England match, I said, "This game doesn't bring out the best in men." Ben responded in a tone that seemed surprised I hadn't noticed this before with, "What sport does?" Hearing him say that warmed my heart. Ben is doing it. He is finding his way to enjoy life and not get sucked into the killer instinct of male sports. He is finding a way of being male while keeping himself emotionally and physically safe.

Maybe I haven't done too badly. Even though fear and ignorance blinded me, I have always assumed that emotions will be part of our relationship, and Ben's relationship with himself. I hope

I have done something to stop the legacy of emotional illiteracy and hunger being passed on to him. Having just assumed that Ben will speak what he feels and say what he needs will, I hope, stop him from continuing the pattern of emotionally unavailable husbands who, like my father and grandfather, didn't hear their wife's needs or recognise that maybe they were in some way responsible. It will also avoid any future daughter-in-law from blaming me for my son's inability to respond to her emotionally. Attention will not become a power play between her and me, because we both feel connected to Ben in our own way. Ben will also not be looking to be mothered by a wife because he hasn't learned to believe that nurturing is only women's work.

Exercises in teaching my son the language of relationships

The underlying theme in mothering sons is that *boys need to be drawn in and held onto*. Girls need more space to fly and breathe on their own, and boys, having been let go of too much, need holding on to in order to help them remain emotionally connected and learn the language of relationships.

As mothers, we have a lot of power to challenge and change The Silent *Male* Scream. We hold the denied emotional language, which means that we hold a large part of the knowledge missing in the cycle that changes our emotionally open young boy into an emotionally illiterate, unavailable man. Helping our boys to keep emotionally connected and supporting them as they navigate the dictates of the male culture saves not just our boys' lives, but also their future relationships, especially with women. It also saves our own life. It will keep us connected to our instinct, to our own emotions, and to our relationships with our sons and the future women in their life. Breaking the cycle has the power to end gender inequality for good, because emotions will no longer be just a female domain, something to be belittled and rejected.

Following are some areas that mothers of sons need to reflect on to make us more aware of the influence we have, in either breaking the cycle or continuing the male culture that so profoundly silences our sons.

• *We have to challenge the culture's messages.*
This means that we have to become educated to the messages that mould our sons and ourselves. We have to start seeing our boys as victims, just like females are, of gender moulding. Boys are victims of a patriarchal system that needs unemotional men to fight, win battles, and make huge amounts of money without recognising the people they kill, walk over, or damage. Dan Kindlon and Michael Thompson suggest, "When male violence is viewed through a different lens, we can come to understand boys better. When an act of vandalism or a violent outburst is seen as a protective response against anticipated pain rather than a biological imperative, we can seek to quell that fear."[36]

• *We have to hold on to our value.*
When we understand the messages, we have far more power to not be bullied into fearing that we are damaging our son, or are holding him back, or being a clingy, demanding kind of mother. We need to remind ourselves and each other that the label "emotionally damaging mother" only applies to mothers who are actually abusive. We also need to redefine the concept of separating from our sons as they enter adulthood. Separating doesn't mean that we walk out of our son's life. It means stepping back gradually and letting him walk on his own, just like we did when he was learning to walk. It means still being there, knowing him, hugging him, and just like with our daughters, developing a mutually supportive relationship.

• *We need to change the conversation that sees men as the enemy.*
In bringing up my son, I have been acutely aware of how my work with women and feminism affects him and my relationship with him. If my attitude to men is that they are the cause of my

disempowerment—the villains—I will firstly be speaking the same language that men speak in casting women as the enemy. Secondly, I will be saying that somehow, Ben, by virtue of his masculinity, is then also the problem, which clearly isn't true. Ben is also a victim of being emotionally disconnected, just as I have been. Casting each other as villains doesn't solve or change anything. It stops us from taking responsibility for our own disempowerment and it doesn't allow the whole picture to emerge, which is essential if the picture is going to be challenged and changed.

• *We need to change the gender-differences conversation.*
It is time that men left Mars and women left Venus, and that we both claim our full humanity here on Earth. I have never felt comfortable with John Gray's title *Men Are From Mars, Women Are From Venus.* In *The Courage To Raise Good Men,* Olga Silverstein and Beth Rashbaum explain that "his *'Vive la difference!'* philosophy is the culture's way of perpetuating the idea of half people, reinforcing our belief that women have access to one set of qualities and abilities, men to another."[37] This conversation leaves both men and women separate and alone. It ignores that, deep down, we are more similar than different, and that we all yearn to be understood and loved. The "difference conversation" is another either/or conversation that can be used to keep men and women in their respective gender boxes. Keeping emotions with women keeps men emotionally isolated in their caves and women feeling neglected with their screams being unheard. Men need to get out of their caves and claim their whole humanity.

• *Mothers need to stop doing all the emotional work.*
If boys are to be expected to get out of their caves and talk, mothers need to stop doing the emotional work for everyone in the family. We need to get out of the way and give our men-folk the space to learn to relate. This will also greatly improve the mother's relationship with her daughter-in-law, because she will

no longer be handing over the emotional work of connecting to her son to her daughter-in-law. As mothers we need to speak anyway, expect to be heard anyway, and to teach our boys a rich emotional language by using it ourselves. We must dig deep and resist the pressure to back off. And of course, this also means that we must challenge any fears we have around men being emotional or "weak," as the cultural message would have us believe.

For me, doing all the emotional work is being the only one the grandparents talk to about what everyone is doing and how we all are, while they only discuss non-relational subjects like money or politics with John. Being the one who gave all the information used to make me feel important, but it's also a burden that often leaves me feeling the messenger. What I can do that doesn't burden me or reduce me is to give encouragement when something needs to be said and isn't. When Ben wanted to hear John tell the story of how he paid too much for a car and John hesitated because he felt too ashamed to tell it, I simply encouraged John to share because it was a golden opportunity for both to connect. I simply told John, "Ben wants to hear your story to understand you more clearly." John later admitted that it healed him to tell the story and show that males don't always get it right.

When boys are allowed to remain in their emotional caves and not taught to be emotionally responsible for themselves and their behaviour, we are in effect making allowance for their non-relational behaviour as if that's what we expect from boys. These boys grow up feeling that they are "entitled princes" who do not have to live by normal relational rules of behaviour. And as men, they will expect their wives and other women to not hold them accountable, just like their mothers. And when they don't get treated as "entitled princes," they won't understand why not. They'll end up feeling confused and angry and let down by women.

I hear many daughters and sisters lament how their brother was their mother's favourite. My brother too was Mum's "golden boy" who could do no wrong. He got away with far more than any of us girls could ever have dreamed of getting away with. This kind of favouritism is highly destructive within a family. It divides mothers and daughters and brothers and sisters. It also puts a huge amount of pressure on the son, who can feel that the mother is living her life through his. This is particularly true when mothers have little life outside the home, and sons and husbands provide the only way of keeping contact with the outside world.

- *Teach our boys to value their full humanity.*
Our boys need a solid inner foundation on which to find a way through the threats, silencing and dangers of the male culture. I agree with Babette Smith, who suggests, "The implications for mothers of sons are that a boy needs to feel confidently masculine *before* he can abhor violence, rather than the other way round."[38] This is a hard task, since the male culture is so very good at teaching self-esteem as having power over, and actively demeaning, any definition of masculinity that doesn't fit into his box. Yet, mothers have power. We can keep holding a different picture for them until they are strong enough and ready to take it on themselves. Telling them often that we value their sensitivity, kindness, and tenderness toward others will keep them in touch with another picture until they are ready to believe it themselves.

In your relationship with your son, ask yourself:

1. When was the last time I told my son how I was really feeling about any topic of conversation?
2. Do I let my son stonewall me whenever I ask him about how he's feeling, how his day was, or about any emotionally laden topic?
3. If so, why? How does it make me feel? How do I imagine it makes my son feel?
4. What can I say the next time he stonewalls or changes the subject?
5. Do I let my son off the hook whenever he's behaving badly? Do I excuse it away as being "typically male"? If so, why?

6. Do I frequently tell my son that I love his sensitivity, kindness, and gentleness toward other people and animals? If not, why not?

7. How do I feel about my son growing up and leaving home? (If your son has already left home, how did you feel about it?)

8. What messages do I have around "letting him go" that have made it more painful and harder to keep in contact?

9. What do I need from my son to make our relationship better?

10. Have I asked for what I need? If not, why not?

11. What messages and fears are stopping me?

I would like to end with a thought of the ocean of tears that mothers silently cry when their boy is torn away from them because she is bullied and threatened to "let him go" and "not stand in his way of becoming a man": tears that are of missing him and yearning to be part of his life, but are silently held inside because she is afraid of being too demanding.

What we also don't hear is the corresponding ocean of tears that boys and men cry because they miss the loving connection with their mum. They too feel bullied into giving up their mothers, at too young an age, when what they needed was her loving understanding, her emotional language, and her warmth and nurturing throughout their entire life.

I wish for mothers that they find the strength to ignore the bullying and keep listening to their mother's heart and keep in touch with their sons. And I wish our sons the courage to begin the long journey of separating their true whole selves from the box they've been bullied into, until piece by piece they claim their full humanity.

20: Claiming My Voice as a Wife and Partner

Women will not enjoy full equality and visibility until
we answer these two key questions: Who is taking care
of the children? Who is taking caring of mum? – RH

I find it fascinating the things that wake us up. Sometimes, it is a throwaway remark that we hear with crystal clarity, or a comment we have heard thousands of times before and then suddenly we hear it as if for the first time, with our hearts. Sometimes we see ourselves reflected in the eyes, lives and stories of others. In those moments we are jolted awake, as if awakened from a coma that has dulled our senses and knowing, and suddenly we can no longer go back to ignoring what we now know and see.

I woke up from the coma I had slipped into as a wife when we sold our home in New Zealand and moved to America, with our two young children in tow, so John could follow his dream of studying for a doctorate. I arrived believing, or probably more accurately, needing to believe that I was happy and contented with my role and place as a wife and mother. I tried not to think that I was following John. I even thought I was a rather liberated wife, having been studying part time toward my bachelor's degree for the past seven years. I also believed that John and I were a partnership, having comatosed my feelings of being alone, all-responsible, and to paraphrase an old saying, left holding the baby four and seven years previously. But as I started looking around at the lives of the women who surrounded me in the eleven-story crescent-shaped apartment block for family student housing on the university campus, my denied truth of my unequal place and voice in my marriage cracked open in an irreparable way.

I could no longer ignore my invisibility, as it stared right back at me. Nor could I return to my comatosed state that had medicated my feelings and managed my periodic surges of anger. I couldn't even cry away my feelings and then pick myself up again and keep going as if nothing had happened, like I used to. Suddenly the status quo didn't feel worth preserving or maintaining anymore. I could no longer swallow the story that I had been told: that, as a wife and mother, I was supposed to support my husband's career, even at my own expense, and be the main nurturer and carer of the family while John followed his dream.

My moment of awakening occurred while I sat on a park bench with other mothers, all non-student spouses, chatting while we watched our children play. As I listened to the women talk again (I had been in this conversation daily since arriving) about their husbands' research interests and how long their degrees were going to take, and where they were hoping to get jobs after graduating, I started to feel my throat close up. I was sick of hearing about their husbands and not about them. I decided to ask them what jobs they had done and what career aspirations they had.

As I asked these questions, they all looked at me with a dull-blank expression in their eyes that communicated that they didn't understand a word I was saying. It was as if I was speaking a foreign language they didn't understand. An uncomfortable silence descended on our little group, until one mother rescued the conversation by resuming the discussion about her husband's job prospects.

I have had this same silent reaction repeat itself in many conversations since, over exactly the same topic: what mothers want.

I was too stunned to be embarrassed that my questions lay unanswered, or that I had created a discomfort in the group. I excused myself, gathered up my children, and went inside to start cooking dinner. But inside me, a storm of disquiet was gathering strength. I knew I was no different from these women. I, too, had moulded my studies around my husband and children, scraping small sections of time for lectures and study so their lives continued, unhindered and unaffected. All of us at the park that day had left family and friends behind, and many of us, homes in other countries, to move with our husband so he could complete his degree with only the vaguest of promise of what his degree would provide for the family. A promise that divorced wives, who supported their husbands through college without investing in their own earning potential, know is rather tenuous: Their husband's future earning potential is an as-yet-unrealised asset wives don't own or have any power or control over.

It was excruciatingly uncomfortable to see my own invisibility and reduced power so starkly reflected back at me. I didn't want to see how I had blindly sacrificed and abdicated my own financial security and confidence in my ability to provide for my family and myself, all relinquished on the promise of my husband's earning potential. I had also suppressed my own career interests and dreams and allowed John to fulfil his whilst ignoring my own. It was also hard to see that this wasn't the first time I had done this. When John studied for his master's degree, I looked after our first child. My level of qualifications at that time was a Trained Teachers' Certificate, which was rather useless because I didn't like being a schoolteacher. In reality, I was qualified for a job I didn't want or like.

Somehow, I had come to accept the conversation that has for generations comatosed wives into believing we do not need to have access to our own financial resources. I had been blinded to a huge inconsistency in the belief that for a man, being financially dependent on his wife is an affront to his masculinity, yet for a woman, being financially dependent on her husband is okay, because dependency is still believed to be a female expectation. And that wasn't all. I was also living with a huge inconsistency between what I believed and what I did. I believed and continue to believe that a woman cannot be completely empowered and confident in herself if she has no access to her own financial resources. Yet I was allowing myself to be financially dependent whilst John increased his earning potential. I had vowed as a teenager and young woman that I wasn't going to repeat the financial dependency, as well as the silent deferral and suppressed sense of identity, that I had seen limit and mark the lives of my mother, grandmother, mother-in-law, and friends' mothers. But somehow, I had fallen into that trap without recognising it.

How did this happen? Maybe I had read too many fairy stories that told me that men, not ourselves, have the power to kiss us awake to ourselves, and that only men have the resources, the knowledge, the castles and armies, and the connections to make things happen? Or was it the messages of duty and sacrifice and selfless caring, along with the nods of approval I received whenever I was being a selfless, caring wife and mother? Was it my mother's message that only selfish, bad mothers and wives work for money, as she spoke the myth that mothers "choose" to work out of their own selfish needs? Did this instil so much guilt that even though I didn't agree with what they all said, I still squeezed my study and work around my family, so as not to hinder them too much with my "selfish" desires to be financially independent and intellectually fulfilled? Or was it my lack of self-belief in my own ability and right to create what I needed and wanted? Was it my "disease to please" that made me overrule my own voice and follow the expectations I heard from my parents and parents-in-law? Or perhaps was it my human need to feel loved, which in my family means behaving in accordance with their standards?

I think all these contributed their own energy to making me disappear from view after I became Mrs. John Hasseldine, though I think not being asked what I wanted, needed, and dreamt of doing after I married had the greatest impact of all. Even more than the passive lack of interest in my wants, needs, and dreams, people started to treat me differently. I was seen as John's wife first and last, and no longer as my own person. And in this process of being invisible, I then became silent to myself and continued to silence myself. Even though I saw through the myths and messages, and had vowed to not repeat the damage I had seen in the women around me, I didn't know how to ask myself what I wanted. Or how to encourage myself to feel entitled to meet my needs and follow my heart's desire. Or how to ask, expect, demand, and claim responsibility for myself, and to share the responsibility for our family. I didn't know that I needed to ask, "What do I need from John?" and "Can he give me what I need?"

A few years after we married, our friend Samantha "dragged" her new husband to the United States so she could study for her doctorate. I remember the disapproval that reverberated around her decision. She was treated by many of the older women in our circle as being selfish, neglectful and demanding, and worse, it was thought she was risking her marriage. I felt jealous of her freedom, but the negative response she got made me unsure, afraid and unclear as to whether I could claim the same freedom. Her sense of liberty inspired me but the disapproval made being so inspired seem dangerous, so I decided to pack the inspiration away. But when John decided to "drag" us to the United States so he could follow his doctoral dream, no one disapproved of or questioned John's decision. Unlike Samantha's husband, I was expected to follow, without question, because as a wife, I was supposed to be supportive.

Not knowing the language that spoke the wisdom in my jealousy, I didn't notice the huge inconsistency between the different reactions until I was shaken awake in the Midwest of the United States. While I watched John skip out the front door to attend lectures, make friends, and feed from the heady mix of terrified excitement that permeates the halls at the start of the academic year, I realised that, once again, I wasn't part of our adventure. Once again, my part and place was to be at home, alone, holding the baby and supporting my husband's dreams. Once again, the myth that we were doing this adventure together, first having a family and now living in a new country, slapped me right across the face, yet this time I felt its false sting.

At first, in my usual way, I picked myself up and tried to get access to facilities the kids and I needed. But at each facility,

I quickly hit a brick wall. I could only get access through John, through his student status. Again, my resources were completely dependent on him. And as I learned to ignore the cockroaches that emerged through the cracks in the kitchen walls, I realised that long ago I had learned that "normal" was to ignore my feelings, needs, and boundaries and the critical and demeaning words, attitudes, and behaviour from others. Normal was putting others' needs and feelings first. Normal was putting up with and adapting myself, just as my grandmother and mother had learned to do. Normal was being in a coma.

But something significant had changed inside of me. Having woken up, I knew I could no longer inhabit my old place. For my own sake, for my children's sake, and for the sake of my relationship with John, I had to reclaim the girl who so strongly wanted to be different, wanted to remain herself, and who wanted to have a strong voice. I had lost myself in not just all the doing and caring for my family, but also through the expectations that instructed and admonished me to believe that being a wife means taking care of your husband and children first.

I started by enrolling in a master's degree program. I wanted to become a counsellor, and I grabbed the chance with both hands. This meant that John's and my arrangement of who did what was going to have to change. Childcare and cooking had to become an equal responsibility. But having done all the cleaning for the first ten years, it seemed fair that it was now John's job for the next ten years. (When I suggest this to clients and they go home and implement this new rule, it is amazing how quickly the money is found to employ a cleaner.)

This all may sound easy, but it wasn't. Handing the cleaning over to John wasn't an easy thing to do. I was like Bree in the television series *Desperate Housewives*. I cleaned to make myself feel better, to feel appreciated, to fill my days, and to create a sense of having a job. Letting John clean the house his way, to his standards, without nagging, reminding, or in desperation doing it anyway, took some time to learn. Each time I snatched it back and did it anyway, I realised that this wasn't letting go. Rather, it only kept me responsible, but with less control than when I did it all. Inside I struggled with the sadness of all my wasted effort to keep the house clean, because I saw now how little it had really been valued. It hurts when all those years you thought that cleaning was showing love and caring and now, when it is someone else's job, the same somehow doesn't apply. It was also very difficult to shrug off the expectation that the standards of cleanliness of my home reflected on me as a wife, mother or homemaker. All women know that this is what everyone automatically thinks: that cleaning is supposed to be the wife's job. It's hard to not buy into this myth and ignore the fear of looking like a failure, a bad wife and mother, in everyone's eyes.

Gradually over the years, a new normal has been created. I learned to let go, and John and I now share the responsibilities of caring for our family far more equally. But equality of responsibility isn't the only thing I require. I also need to feel that John knows me on an emotional level, and I need to feel I know him. I need to feel that he knows what I am feeling and thinking: to be asked how my day has been, and that he values my reply. I also need to know what's going on for him. I am wired to think in terms of relationships, and knowing him and being known by him is what I, what all women need. When this conversation is missing, our relationship feels cold, empty and uncaring. It feels like we're reduced to a well-oiled machine that runs the family with great efficiency, without the warmth of relating as a couple, partners, soul mates and lovers. In the juggling of the family, the "us" and "I" of who we are is so easily drowned out.

"It is so hard to know what a woman wants" is bandied about so often, it's treated as if it speaks a well-known fact that women are so complex, knowing what we need is an unanswerable quest. This is rubbish! It is a myth that tries to make discovering what women want a waste of time. It is a red herring that diverts our attention from recognising the lack of respect there is for women's voices. As I listen to women talk about their relationships with men, I see no mystery to what women want. What I repeatedly hear is that we want to feel loved, cherished, valued and known. Like all human beings, we want to be known.

I witness on a daily basis the soul abuse that women suffer when they are treated as the invisible, unseen carers of their family. I see their heartbreaking loneliness, confusion, self-doubt, and increasing self-silencing as they begin to mirror the same invisibility in their relationship with themselves. I grew up witnessing the loneliness that swirled around Grandmother and Mother. I didn't understand it then as I do now. I didn't know then that they were suffering from relational invisibility, which left them alone and sad and next to, and in my grandmother's case, behind her husband. Alone with their feelings, words, thoughts, and needs, all locked up inside with no ability to speak or feel heard.

I don't know if my father and grandfather saw the lonely sadness that was so obvious to me, or how they explained it to themselves in their heads. To me they seemed rather oblivious and detached from their wives, treating their feelings, and especially their sadness as if it was due to some mysterious female condition, and therefore, completely unrelated and irrelevant to them. I never saw them go up to their wife and gently ask her how she was. I suppose they never saw their fathers emotionally engaging with their wives. They were both very much a part of the generation that saw themselves as the providers of their family in the traditional sense of the word and their wives as the nurturer and carer of them all. Dad didn't realise his relationship with Mum needed tending with the same dedication he tended his vegetables, and that she needed him to be emotionally present and available. Neither of them knew that relational invisibility is abusive and spirit crushing.

I guess my mother and grandmother also didn't understand that they were suffering from relational invisibility. They had learned to think that the only question they needed to ask was how well a man could provide financially. This was an important question for them to answer, because they had learned to believe they couldn't provide for themselves, even though my Grandmother was a chemist just like Grandfather and my mother had a professional qualification, whereas my father barely finished high school. Both could've earned as much, if not more, than their husbands. But I am not talking about financial support here. Too many women still don't know that we need to ask ourselves, "*What emotional needs do I need my boyfriend, husband or partner to meet?*" And having answered that, we need to ask, *"Can he give me what I need?"*

Too often, when I talk to women about these questions, they get a confused blankness in their eyes. It hits them like a completely unheard-of concept, and is, until they think about it for a while and realise that not knowing the answers to these questions is a large part of their emotionally starved landscape.

We have learned to switch ourselves off instead of knowing that we matter too and that relationships are a mutual exchange of being heard and known. We need to be nurtured within our relationships just as much as we need to nurture ourselves. We haven't woken up to the fact that being loved should not be earned by giving and giving. Being loved is a given that we deserve to feel just because we exist, and all we have to do is ask for it, expect it, and put up with nothing less.

As my mind flicks through my current clients, I realise that every single one of them has either just left, is thinking of leaving, or is struggling to stay in relationships in which they are emotionally neglected. And they have each had one or two emotionally neglectful parents. Not a coincidence, I think! These women are waking up to the knowledge that they need the simple life-giving energy of being heard, valued and cherished. I too am recovering from being an emotionally neglected wife and partner. I am learning to put up with nothing less than being equally visible, and I am glad John is responding well to my awakening. I don't think our relationship would've survived if he had resisted my need for change. He too is waking up and realising his male myths and stereotypes don't fit with what he needs. We have both become lost in the busy years of parenting our children, jobs, the denial that women have needs, and the expectations that men must achieve and provide. John and I have some catching up to do. Every day now, we take the time to ask each other how our day has been. I have a hunch that, for women, feeling known and loved is a much stronger aphrodisiac than any potion or oysters.

I know things are changing, not just because I am feeling different, but because our daughter said to me as we were driving in the car, "Dad is good at the romantic stuff." In reality, what she was commenting on was that John was organising a "mystery getaway" for the two of us for the first time. Even so, I heard hope in her voice. I heard that she was noticing and wondering how she might like to be treated by her future boyfriend or partner. The question "What do I need?" had sprouted in her mind. She was also showing the powerful role husbands play in changing or maintaining the silent invisibility of mothers. How men treat the mother of their daughter and son will leave an impression of what women can expect. But we cannot wait and hope that our husbands or partners will change. If women don't react when we are suffering from emotional neglect or relational invisibility, we are showing our children that neglect of women is normal.

Exercises to claim my equal place and visibility as a wife and partner

Ask yourself:

1. What do I need from my boyfriend/husband/partner?
2. Have I told him what I need?
3. Am I communicating my needs and feelings without self-doubt in my voice?
4. Do I feel that he hears my needs and communicates that he values them?
5. If not, what is happening in the relationship that is leaving me feeling unheard?
6. What beliefs do my partner and I have about a wife and husband's roles and value? How are these beliefs influencing the decisions I make, the power I have, and the jobs I do?
7. What beliefs are empowering and supportive, and disempowering and unsupportive, of me and of my partner/husband?

8. What stories are hidden in my family's and in-laws'
    closets that put wives down and silence my needs
    and feelings?

Here is why all these questions are important, but particularly the
ones about beliefs and stories the reader might be acting upon,
subconsciously or not. Questions 9 & 10 will follow:

The beliefs and stories families hold onto and then act out from
are powerful, so powerful, they can prevent us from sensing,
much less being able or willing to ask for what we need. These
beliefs and stories can be a belief like, "All women are best at
caring for children and cleaning." Another one: "Women are
emotional beings that you can't understand." Yet another one, and
one that is in my in-laws' and my own family is, "Women are a
little crazy and unfulfilled if they don't have a child."

There is also the story of how wives "cut their husbands off in their
prime" by refusing to have sex. When the story is told, they talk
about how sorry they feel for the husband, and his wife is painted as
emotionally unstable, deficient, selfish, and unloving, and a "ball-
crusher." No one asks what was happening for her in the relationship
that led her to make this decision. And they definitely don't cheer her
on with any sort of "good for her" phrasing for standing up for her
right to say no. She is perceived to have no right to say no.

The powerful messages in these beliefs and stories are of male
control, fear of not being able to control a strong-minded wife,
and the dread of looking like a weak, henpecked male. These
messages also assume that wives don't own their own minds,
bodies, or sexuality.

9. How are all the chores and domestic duties
    divided up? How does that division of labour
    feel to me? Am I happy with it, or does something
    irritate me or make me resentful?
    (Don't "yes but" any answers you come up with.
    Let your soul speak how you really feel.)
    When John and I married, it was just assumed that

I would do all the domestic duties, just as my mother and his mother had done. I assumed it too, without any questions. I didn't know to ask, *"What are we each going to do to contribute to the running of our home?"* Taking care of our home felt like my way of showing love and care. What was missing was that I hadn't learned to ask, *"What do I need John to take responsibility for so that I too feel cared for?"*

10. Since many women are in paid employment and have careers, how are your respective jobs and careers treated? Are they treated with equal value, or is one treated as more valuable? How does earning potential influence which job or career gets more value? How does childcare influence which job or career gets more value?

21: Claiming My Voice with My Female Friends

We betray each other, every time a woman criticises another for stepping out of her prescribed box or speaking her truth. We betray each other, every time a woman doesn't support another's growth or omits to stick up for her when she is being silenced. Being criticised by men hurts, but being criticised by women hurts even more. It cuts away at the sisterhood that our hearts need and our souls yearn for. – RH

Some of my female friendships didn't survive my awakening. When I was in my "do what it takes" and "being nice means being liked" mode of thinking, my friends had no problems with me. They liked that I was quietly supportive, not demanding, and eager to work around them. The stronger my voice became, the less some of my friends liked it. Just as Lauren predicted and Jill discovered when she said no (See chapter 3 "Taught to Be Silent"), some of my female friends didn't like it when I started to say no, to speak my needs, or to say when I was feeling hurt by their behaviour. Suddenly I was being accused of becoming aggressive, unfriendly or unhelpful. Some said so; others communicated their dislike with silent withdrawal.

At first their reactions hurt, but as I thought about it, I realised that the relationships that didn't survive were the ones in which I had lost my voice. They were the ones in which I felt anxious at the thought of speaking, where my tears were ignored and my no was responded to with anger. In short, they were the relationships in which I had to choose between speaking and being loved, between honouring myself and keeping the relationship. It took my awakening to realise that I had been hushing my awareness of being invisible with worries that I was being paranoid about possible negative reactions. But I wasn't being paranoid. My fears were right. They were warning me that speaking wasn't welcome in these relationships.

Why wasn't my voice welcome? Why is it so hard for some women to hear another woman empower herself? Why did Mum and some of my friends feel so threatened by my emerging self? Why had Lauren learned that other females don't like it when she speaks? Why wasn't Jill's "No" celebrated? Why is my suggestion that mothers have needs and are entitled to their own lives frequently greeted with defensive anger? And why is this book riddled with stories of women silencing each other: women failing to enquire after each other and only enquiring as to how the woman's child and husband are? Or a granddaughter having her feelings shamed by her grandmother, or a daughter being silenced and ignored by her mother and mother-in-law. Or, a woman having her knowledge silenced by her supervisor, and her sisters, friends, and colleagues reacting with anger when a woman speaks her mind or sets her boundaries?

These are only a few stories of many. We have all heard about women accusing each other of being "needy," "selfish," "demanding," "uncaring," "unprofessional," or "not a team player." I have heard many baffling stories of how harsh a critic other mothers can be. Even though mothers experience a high degree of "shaming blame," they can sometimes be the worst offenders. They shush each other's voices and guilt-trip other mothers with, "Your children are only young once, enjoy them while you can," or "Surely you love your children!" The women in my family "eye-roll," or ask the "Yes but, what about your kids?" question, or worse, give the "silent look of disapproval" that clearly communicates when they dislike my mothering choices: choices like expecting John to cook, clean, and take care of the kids and my not having the evening meal prepared by nine in the morning. (No, I am not kidding. Having dinner organised by nine in the morning is expected in my family.)

Why do so many clients say "Oh, no!" when I ask them if they have told another girl or woman that they (the girl or woman) have upset them? Why do they respond in a tone of surprise that I would even suggest this? The reasons they give usually fall within the following list:

- I don't think I will be understood.
- I don't want to be a burden.
- I'm afraid of upsetting the other person.
- I'm afraid my words will be turned against me.
- I'm afraid of losing the friendship.

I also hear stories of women silencing their achievements out of fear of making their girlfriends jealous. Many of us know how poisonous jealousy can be to a relationship, so we downplay great news like a new job or a new relationship. Jealousy seems to be rife amongst women, and because we have been trained to be "nice," women keep quiet so to avoid upsetting their friends and spoiling the relationship by awakening jealousy.

What is going on between women? Something is obviously blocking us from speaking and hearing each other's voices, supporting each other to speak anyway, and cheering each other on to "go for it." If we go back to our primary female relationship, the mother-daughter relationship, we know that when we deny a mother's needs, this can create jealousy and conflict. (See chapter 17 "Claiming My Voice as a Mother.) It makes sense that this is also happening in our other female relationships. *Being taught to be "good" and silent damages our relationship with ourselves, and our relationship with other females. Our emotional starvation disables our ability to hear and value each other's voices. And being starved makes needs, attention, and "go for it" a battle, a competition, and a painful thing to witness in other women.*

This is what blocked my friends' ability to embrace my awakening. Their own silence made it uncomfortable for them to hear my needs and feelings, and especially my anger. I was voicing the same feelings they were struggling to hear and feel entitled to.

My awakening was holding up an uncomfortable mirror. But instead of learning from it, they chose to return to the all-too-familiar "nice" female mould and criticise me for stepping out of it.

If being silent is the only conversation we know, we will continue that silence in the conversations we have with other women. We will silence ourselves and discourage other women from speaking the feelings and needs we don't feel entitled to speak ourselves. Our female relationships are particularly vulnerable to this type of contamination, because our silence is so bound up with being female. We are particularly vulnerable to passing on our emotional disconnection and starvation to each other, and also to catching it from each other, because our female relationships are so important to our well-being. We mirror for each other what it means to be female, whether a silent female or an empowered, entitled female.

Sadly, what I am describing can turn rather nasty between women and girls. Our discomfort about our daughter, sister, granddaughter, girlfriend, or colleague speaking the very feelings, thoughts, needs, and dreams we have learned to deny but our souls are screaming for can create an undercurrent of jealousy, criticism, anger, and resentment. It can create an emotionally violent current that ripples under the surface between females, because we don't know how to own or speak our truth aloud.

In our female relationships is where the political becomes very personal. The jealousy women feel toward each other is a by-product of our socialisation for silence. Understanding this is key to decontaminating our female relationships. If we know we've been *taught* to feel jealous, we can stop blaming ourselves for feeling jealous and instead spend our energy on understanding why. We can start listening to our jealousy as a warning that our souls are missing something important, that it is human, natural and even healthy to feel jealous of another female claiming the very things we've been taught to deny. How can this not make us feel jealous?

Once we understand our reactions, we have so much more power to heal ourselves and claim the voices our souls are screaming to speak. We will be less likely to shame ourselves and give into the desire to punish other women for showing us what we are missing. Criticising women is a familiar language. We hear it spoken every day. I hear too many girls and women tell painful stories of how their girlfriends and sisters tried to tear them down in the hope of having them give up their newfound empowerment. I passed on a piece of my inner silence to my own daughter, Olivia when I questioned the motives behind her teacher's glowing respect for her work. I realised what I had done when I saw worry erase the joy in her eyes. My heart sank. How could I do this when I was completely delighted about her well-deserved success and recognition? Why did I tear down the recognition she so deserved? Why were my mother's put-downs coming out of my own mouth, when I so clearly remember the power they had to reduce my self-worth?

Something was clearly bothering me. After some reflection, I realised that in her praise and recognition from her teacher, I saw the lack of recognition I was getting for my mother-daughter-relationship work from some of my colleagues. Her pleasure reminded me of how unrecognised I was feeling. But instead of pausing to own my own feelings so I could celebrate her different experience, I reduced her self-enhancing enjoyment. Whatever my reasons, it wasn't okay to tear away Olivia's happiness and sow seeds of doubt to protect myself from my own discomfort. Here, right before me, I saw how my relationship with my daughter and my daughter's relationship with herself could be damaged when I don't own and voice what *I* need. But first, before I looked at myself, I had to apologise to Olivia and explain to her that what I said wasn't about her, but totally and completely about me. By claiming it back, I hope I restored her pleasure for her well-deserved success.

The truth is that every time we silence or criticise each other, we are betraying each other. We are continuing and reinforcing the norm that has made it okay to silence females, to question our truth, to criticise our choices, and turn our basic feelings and needs around as symptomatic of some female pathology. Every time we use the same questions, the same criticisms and the same conversations that silence, we are normalising and aiding and abetting our training for silence. This training silences our anger and the creation of a conversation that owns and apologises for our behaviour.

Though I believe that the world is changed one woman at a time, our journey to claiming our voices and creating relationships in which we are fully heard needs to be encircled by the support of other women. We need to stand together to create a strongly woven, multicoloured protective wall that speaks all the different shades of what being female is. We each need to feel the strength of women standing behind us. We need to feel our mothers, grandmothers, friends and other wise women standing behind us, urging us to "go for it" and reminding us who we are in those moments when we've forgotten. We need to create and find emotionally safe, mutually empowering relationships in which we encourage each other to speak anyway and to "go for it," whatever that goal might be.

Without this wall of female wisdom, stories, caring, nurturing and belonging, we are each alone. Even more, we will feel a draught on our backs that will make us anxious about whether we're doing okay. I needed my mother, sister and girlfriends to surround me after I gave birth to my children. I needed them to help me celebrate my power to give birth, to help me talk out the trauma of the experience, and to gather my son, my daughter and I into our collective female power. We need each other to help us mark and gain wisdom at those moments in our lives. We also need the wisdom from those women who are travelling ahead of us.

When I turned forty, I suddenly craved contact with older women. Every time I spotted a strong and wise-looking woman in her fifties or sixties, I wanted to rush up to her and ask her what it was like being her age. I wanted to know the wisdom she had collected as I journeyed into the next stage of my life. This is why claiming our voices is revolutionary work! The claiming has the power to heal the wounds inflicted by generations of silence and to help us speak our voices in our female relationships. Just as we can learn to deny our voices through our friends' criticism, we can also learn to know and accept our voices when we see them reflected in our mother's eyes and our girlfriend's eyes and hear ourselves reflected in their stories. I am always amazed how much calmer and stronger I feel after I have put the world to right with my girlfriends. I come away feeling more at home with myself.

The Silent Female Scream (www.thesilentfemalescream.com) is a revolution that empowers women and girls to connect with themselves and each other, and as mothers and daughters. As with other female-led revolutions, like those led by the suffragettes, when women gather to empower themselves and each other, a great wave of entitlement is unleashed that will not take no for an answer, a mighty and massive wave that will not subside until our voices have been heard and are treated as normal. The good news is that we already have the skills to create this revolution. We have the relational skills of listening, caring, nurturing and empathy engendering that we use in the care of others, including our husbands, families and children. All we have to do is claim them back for ourselves.

It is also important to be aware of the unacknowledged undercurrent of fear around women claiming their power. But just focusing on this and blaming society or men for our disempowerment won't help us. We have to look at our own fear of being powerful. Soon after I arrived in the United States, I was invited to a "wild women's weekend." I had never been to such a gathering, had never witnessed seeing naked women of all shapes and sizes step boldly, without shame, into the hot tub and talk and talk until they were wrinkled and dried out. It was both thrilling and scary. It was also my first encounter with tarot cards, and it was wonderful to see these women come together as themselves in such an activity. Yet it also scared me. These women showed me how little I owned my femaleness, my power, and my being. But having had a glimpse, I wanted more of this. I wanted to be like these bold, uncritical women and gather with other bold, uncritical women.

We are all on a journey of claiming a new way of expressing our female power, a power that builds and connects, listens and speaks, heals and lifts and holds a place for all our voices, including when we are angry at each other. I don't feel we yet have all the answers to what female power is going to be like, because after generations of having our power silenced or burnt at the stake, it is all very new. What I do know is that, in this new model, we have to be exceedingly careful that it doesn't turn into another form of "being nice and getting along," as Naomi Wolf warns.[39] We have to be free to compete, to win, to want to be the best, and to also want that for each other. We need to be free to empower ourselves and each other without undermining each other's autonomy.

I remember how freeing it was to be part of a women's group facilitated by a female minister. It was so energising, like breathing in clean air, to be free to say whatever I thought, to just voice a belief or train of thought, and to have the space to change my mind at any time. No one criticised, questioned or shushed anyone for saying something they didn't believe in or thought was inappropriate. It is interesting that I don't recall a lot of conflict in this group. We didn't have to fight with each other to have our voices heard. And this wasn't a group you could come and dump all your woes on, or use to absolve your responsibility for your life. Women who complained a lot and needed buckets of sympathy without wanting to be challenged to take charge of their life didn't stay long. Honestly, it was a relief when they left. Their victim-like presence sucked all the fresh air out of the room.

Part of creating a new feminine voice is becoming angry. Anger is a healthy reaction when our collective femininity has been hurt and a wonderful catalyst for change. I am talking about an anger that understands that mothers, grandmothers, girlfriends and colleagues are so silent, and their silence has become so entrenched, they don't know anything different. I am angry about my family's legacy of complete female silence. I am very sad thinking how this has decimated my relationship with my mother and sister. I am angry that I sat all alone in my hospital bed with my new daughter, and I feel bad that Mum and I didn't go and celebrate my sister when she had her children. It makes me sad that no one said how important it was that we gather at these events. I am angry that no one noticed the connection between my new daughter's difficulty with sleeping and feeding and my postnatal depression. Looking back, it is so obvious that both of us were screaming our individual and collective emotional neglect. It also makes me angry that Jill's first "No" was met with such strong resistance. And I feel incredibly sad for those women who are so alone and neglected, they don't know what to do when a nurturing voice finds them. Nurturing is so unfamiliar to them, they reject it because its unfamiliarity frightens them.

I will leave you with a final thought about being our own cheerleader and finding a good cheerleader. Finding a good cheerleader starts with ourselves, as Joan Anderson discovered in *A Year by the Sea*: "Tonight I shall open a can of soup and dine happily alone. I'm learning to sponsor myself, no longer the servant but a master of my own time and destiny."[40]

There is such power in time alone. It restores the flow of receiving and giving as we learn to give to ourselves and receive from ourselves. We also need a good mentor who isn't invested in how we live our life. A mother can make a wonderful mentor if she's strong enough to allow her daughter to be fully herself. But whether we are lucky to have such a mother, or we don't, we still need a circle of women who will help us dust ourselves off, learn our life lessons, and continue following our voices and respective paths.

Thank you for reading my story and the voices of the brave women who helped tell its message.

I wish you all a good journey in finding your voices and claiming your birthright to speak your truth with strength, conviction, and clarity.

Go well with love and peace

Rosjke Hasseldine

Exercises in speaking my true voice with my female friends

Reflect on your female relationships and ask yourself:

1. Can I remember incidents where I was afraid to speak, or my feelings and needs were silenced?
2. How was I silenced?
3. How did it affect me?
4. How did it affect my relationship with myself?
5. What do I need to do to build a strong protection against being silenced?
6. Can I remember incidents when someone else's feelings and needs irritated me and I silenced them?
7. How did I silence them?
8. How did it affect me?
9. How did it affect my relationship with them?
10. What is this incident showing me that I need to claim for myself?
11. Am I part of a supportive female network? If not, why not? What relationships am I putting up with that that aren't supportive of me?
12. Do I have a good mentor? If not, what do I need to do to find one?
13. What female rituals and celebrations have been lost in my family and with my girlfriends? How can I reclaim them as part of my daily, monthly, and seasonal lifecycle?

Notes

Part 1: Taught to Be Silent
1. Pipher, M. (1994). *Reviving Ophelia: Saving the Selves of Adolescent Girls.* (New York: Grosset/Putnam), p. 22.
2. Lauren is one of the girls in the study by Brown, L. M. and Gilligan, C. (1992). *Meeting at the Crossroads: Women's Psychology and Girls' Development.* (Cambridge MA: Harvard), p. 73.
3. Brown, L. M. and Gilligan, C. (1992). *Meeting at the Crossroads: Women's Psychology and Girls' Development.* (Cambridge MA: Harvard), p. 80.
4. Northrup, C. (1994). *Women's Bodies, Women's Wisdom: Creating Physical and Emotional Health and Healing.* (New York: Bantam), p. 427.
5. Simmons, R. (2002). *Odd Girl Out: The Hidden Culture of Aggression in Girls.* (New York: Harcourt), p. 106.
6. Wolf, N. (1993). *Fire with Fire: The New Female Power and How It Will Change the 21st Century.* (New York: Random House), p. 236.
7. Wolf, N. (1993). *Fire with Fire: The New Female Power and How It Will Change the 21st Century.* (New York: Random House), p. 240.

No One is Taking Care of Mum
8. Wolf, N. (2001). *Misconceptions: Truth, Lies and the Unexpected on the Journey to Motherhood.* (London: Chatto & Windus), pp. 193–194.

Where is Our Female Story?
9. Estés, C. P. (1998). *Women Who Run With the Wolves.* (London: Rider), pp. 377 & 383.

Why Do We Tolerate Being Silenced?
10. Wolf, N. (1993). *Fire with Fire: The New Female Power and How It Will Change the 21st Century.* (New York: Random House), p. 236.

Part 2: Claiming My Emotional Needs
11.   Baber, K. M. and Allen, K. R. (1992). *Women & Families: Feminist Reconstructions.* (New York: The Guilford Press), p. 152.

Claiming My Feelings and Anger
12.   Simmons, R. (2002). *Odd Girl Out: The Hidden Culture of Aggression in Girls.* (New York: Harcourt), pp. 153–154.
13.   Wolf, N. (1993). *Fire with Fire: The New Female Power and How It Will Change the 21st Century.* (New York: Random House), p. 288.

Claiming My Availability for Myself
14.   Northrup, C. (2001). *The Wisdom of Menopause: The Complete Guide to Creating Physical and Emotional Health and Healing.* (London: Piatkus), p. 19.
15.   Braun Levine, S. (2005). *Inventing the Rest of Our Lives: Women in Second Adulthood.* (London: Viking), p. 89.
16.   Lerner, H. (1986). *The Dance of Anger: A Woman's Guide to Changing the Patterns of Intimate Relationships.* (New York: Harper & Row Publishers, Inc.), p. 6.

Claiming and Healing My Wounds
17.   Rosenberg, M. B. (2003). *Non-violent Communication: A Language of Life.* (Encinitas, CA: PuddleDancer), pp. 57–61.
18.   Carolyn Myss workshop entitled *"The sacred contract of the healer. Nurturing yourself in the midst of service"* 18 April 2004, London. Organised by Hay House.

Claiming My Body
19.   Northrup, C. (1994). *Women's Bodies, Women's Wisdom: Creating Physical and Emotional Health and Healing.* (New York: Bantam), p. 567.

20. Wolf, N. (1991). *The Beauty Myth.* (London: Vintage), p. 184.
21. Northrup, C. (2005). *Mother-Daughter Wisdom: Creating a Legacy of Physical and Emotional Health.* (London: Piatkus), p. 103.
22. Northrup, C. (2005). *Mother-Daughter Wisdom: Creating a Legacy of Physical and Emotional Health.* (London: Piatkus), p. 103.
23. Northrup, C. (2005). *Mother-Daughter Wisdom: Creating a Legacy of Physical and Emotional Health.* (London: Piatkus), p. 84.
24. Northrup, C. (2005). *Mother-Daughter Wisdom: Creating a Legacy of Physical and Emotional Health.* (London: Piatkus), p. 21.
25. Northrup, C. (1994). *Women's Bodies, Women's Wisdom: Creating Physical and Emotional Health and Healing.* (New York: Bantam), p. 287.
26. Northrup, C. (1994). *Women's Bodies, Women's Wisdom: Creating Physical and Emotional Health and Healing.* (New York: Bantam), p. 288.

Part 3: Claiming My Voice as My Mother's Daughter

27. Bassoff, E. S. (1992). *Mothering Ourselves: Help and Healing for Adult Daughters.* (New York: Plume), p. 31.

Claiming My Voice as a Mother

28. Wolf, N. (2001). *Misconceptions: Truth, Lies and the Unexpected on the Journey to Motherhood.* (London: Chatto & Windus), p. 204.
29. Buchanan, A. J. (2003). *Mother Shock: Loving Every (Other) Minute of It.* (New York: Seal), p. 66.
30. The Association for Research on Mothering (ARM) 8th annual conference—*Mothering and Feminism* Conference, October 22–24 2004, York University, Toronto. www.yorku.ca/arm

31. Pearson, A. (2003). *I Don't Know How She Does It.* (London: Vintage).
32. www.askDrSears.com. *The Shutdown Syndrome.* November 2004.

Claiming My Voice as My Son's Mother

33. Smith, B. (1995). *Mothers & Sons.* (Sydney: Allen & Unwin), p. 222.
34. Smith, B. (1995). *Mothers & Sons.* (Sydney: Allen & Unwin), p. 7.
35. Kindlon, D. and Thompson, M. (2000). *Raising Cain: Protecting the Emotional Life of Boys.* (New York: Ballantine), p. xix.
36. Kindlon, D. and Thompson, M. (2000). *Raising Cain: Protecting the Emotional Life of Boys.* (New York: Ballantine), p. 237.
37. Silverstein, O. & Rashbaum, B. (1994). *The Courage to Raise Good Men: You Don't Have to Sever the Bond with your Son to Help Him Become a Man.* (New York: Penguin), p. 203.
38. Smith, B. (1995). *Mothers & Sons.* (Sydney: Allen & Unwin), p. 71.

Claiming My Voice with My Female Friends

39. Wolf, N. (1993). *Fire with Fire: The New Female Power and How It will Change the 21st Century.* (New York: Random House), p. 261.
40. Anderson, J. (2000). *A Year by the Sea: Thoughts of an Unfinished Woman.* (New York: Broadway Books), p. 123.

Bibliography

Anderson, J. (2000). *A Year by the Sea: Thoughts of an Unfinished Woman.* (New York: Broadway Books).

Arcana, J. (1981). *Our Mothers' Daughters.* (London: The Women's Press).

Arcana, J. (1983). *Every Mother's Son: The Role of Mothers in the Making of Men.* (London: The Women's Press).

Baber, K. M. and Allen, K. R. (1992). *Women & Families: Feminist Reconstructions.* (New York: The Guilford Press).

Bassoff, E. S. (1992). *Mothering Ourselves: Help and Healing for Adult Daughters.* (New York: Plume).

Braun Levine, S. (2005). *Inventing the Rest of Our Lives: Women in Second Adulthood.* (London: Viking).

Bronte, C. (1992). *Jane Eyre.* (London: Wordsworth).

Brown, L. M. and Gilligan, C. (1992). *Meeting at the Crossroads: Women's Psychology and Girls' Development.* (Cambridge MA: Harvard).

Buchanan, A. J. (2003). *Mother Shock: Loving Every (Other) Minute of It.* (New York: Seal).

Caplan, P. J. (2000). *The New Don't Blame Mother: Mending the Mother-Daughter Relationship.* (London: Routledge).

Dowling, C. (1981). *The Cinderella Complex: Women's Hidden Fear of Independence.* (New York: Summit).

Ensler, E. (2001). *The Vagina Monologues.* (London: Virago).

Estés, C. P. (1998). *Women Who Run With the Wolves.* (London: Rider).

Faludi, S. (1999). *Stiffed: The Betrayal of the Modern Man.* (London: Chatto & Windus).

Fox, F. (2003). *Dispatches From a Not-So-Perfect Life: Or How I Learned to Love the House, the Man, the Child.* (New York: Harmony).

Friedan, B. (1965). *The Feminine Mystique.* (London: Penguin).

Gilligan, C. (1993). *In a Different Voice: Psychological Theory and Women's Development.* (Cambridge MA: Harvard).

Gray, J. (1992). *Men Are From Mars, Women Are From Venus.* (London: HarperCollins).

Greer, G. (2000). *The Whole Woman.* (London: Anchor).

Hay, L. L. (1999). *You Can Heal Your Life.* (Carlsbad CA: Hay House).

Hendrix, H. (1988). *Getting the Love You Want.* (New York: Henry Holt).

Hirschmann, J. R. and Munter, C. H. (1995). *When Women Stop Hating Their Bodies: Freeing Yourself From Food and Weight Obsession.* (New York: Fawcett Columbine).

Jeffers, S. (1987). *Feel the Fear and Do It Anyway.* (London: Arrow).

Jong, E. (2000). *What Do Women Want?* (London: Bloomsbury).

Kindlon, D. and Thompson, M. (2000). *Raising Cain: Protecting the Emotional Life of Boys.* (New York: Ballantine).

Lerner, H. (1986). *The Dance of Anger: A Woman's Guide to Changing the Patterns of Intimate Relationships.* (New York: Harper & Row Publishers, Inc.).

van Mens-Verhulst, J., Schreurs, K., and Woertman, L. (eds). (1993). *Daughtering and Mothering: Female Subjectivity Reanalysed.* (London: Routledge).

Myss, C. (1996). *Anatomy of the Spirit: The Seven Stages of Power and Healing.* (New York: Three Rivers Press).

Northrup, C. (1994). *Women's Bodies, Women's Wisdom: Creating Physical and Emotional Health and Healing.* (New York: Bantam).

Northrup, C. (2001). *The Wisdom of Menopause: The Complete Guide to Creating Physical and Emotional Health and Healing.* (London: Piatkus).

Northrup, C. (2005). *Mother-Daughter Wisdom: Creating a Legacy of Physical and Emotional Health.* (London: Piatkus).

O'Donohue, J. (1997). *Anam Cara: Spiritual Wisdom from the Celtic World.* (London: Bantam).

Olsen, T. (2003) *Silences.* (New York: Feminist Press at the City University of New York).

Orbach, S. and Eichenbaum, L. (2000). *What Do Women Want?* (London: HarperCollins).

Orenstein, P. (1994). *School Girls: Young Women, Self-Esteem and the Confidence Gap.* (New York: Anchor).

Pearson, A. (2003). *I Don't Know How She Does It.* (London: Vintage).

Peskowitz, M. (2005). *The Truth Behind the Mommy Wars: Who Decides What Makes a Good Mother?* (Emeryville CA: Seal).

Pipher, M. (1994). *Reviving Ophelia: Saving the Selves of Adolescent Girls.* (New York: Grosset/Putnam).

Rich, A. (1977). *Of Woman Born.* (London: Virago).

Rosenberg, M. B. (2003). *Non-Violent Communication: A Language of Life.* (Encinitas, CA: PuddleDancer).

Secunda, V. (1992). *When You and Your Mother Can't Be Friends: Resolving the Most Complicated Relationship of Your Life.* (London: Cedar).

Shandler, N. (2002). *Ophelia's Mum: Women Speak Out About Loving and Letting Go of Their Adolescent Daughters.* (London: Vermilion).

Shandler, S. (1999). *Ophelia Speaks: Adolescent Girls Write About Their Search for Self.* (New York: HarperCollins).

Silverstein, O. & Rashbaum, B. (1994). *The Courage to Raise Good Men: You Don't Have to Sever the Bond With Your Son to Help Him Become a Man.* (New York: Penguin).

Simmons, R. (2002). *Odd Girl Out: The Hidden Culture of Aggression in Girls.* (New York: Harcourt).

Smith, B. (1995). *Mothers & Sons.* (Sydney: Allen & Unwin).

Williamson, M. (1993). *A Woman's Worth.* (New York: Ballantine).

Wiseman, R. (2002). *Queen Bees & Wannabes: Helping Your Daughter Survive Cliques, Gossip, Boyfriends & Other Realities of Adolescence.* (London: Piatkus).

Wolf, N. (1991). *The Beauty Myth.* (London: Vintage).

Wolf, N. (1993). *Fire with Fire: The New Female Power and How It will Change the 21st Century.* (New York: Random House).

Wolf, N. (2001). *Misconceptions: Truth, Lies and the Unexpected on the Journey To Motherhood.* (London: Chatto & Windus).

Wollstonecraft, M. (2004). *A Vindication of the Rights of Woman.* (London: Penguin).

Woolf, V. (1998). *A Room of One's Own and Three Guineas.* (Oxford: Oxford World's Classics).

Acknowledgements

This book would not have been born without the nurturing support of a number of great people. John, my partner, husband and soul mate. Thank you for your endless patience and proof reading. Your unfailing encouragement has helped me keep my eye on the goal. You have walked with me on this journey and your steadfast love and belief in my ideas and passion to write, have sustained me. Thank you for carrying the responsibility for the family's financial resources. I hope that soon I can return the favour.

Ben and Olivia, thank you for teaching me about what we need to feel nurtured, heard, and loved and for your support and love.

All our relationships are sent to teach us about ourselves. Thank you to my friends and the many women and men who have helped me wake-up.

Rev Edwin Clarke, thank you for being the first to teach me to stand back and question how I was allowing myself to be treated. You helped me start thinking that maybe I could create an emotional life that wasn't limited by silence or shaped by those who were threatened by my voice. I said to you that I would acknowledge you in my first book. Now finally, twenty years later, here it is.

Amy Sutley, my dear friend, thank you for your gentle supportive encouragement. Your emails and telephone calls were always well timed and they always held the power to re-ignite the spark of possibility that I had temporarily lost sight of. My relationship with you is very precious. Thank you for teaching me to hear my writing voice with clarity, for your heart-felt wisdom, and the many books you mailed to me.

Arlene Robinson, my wonderful editor, I am so glad I found you. Thank you for your great editorial skills. You are a gifted editor. You polished my words with such care and grace and you fed a tender writer's heart with a reflection of my work that I hadn't yet dared to believe as true.

Ele Pack, my gifted artist. Thank you for your beautiful painting and creating the image that I had carried around in my head for so many years.

Thank you to all the courageous women who have contributed to my learning and writing about women's emotional silencing. Your stories and struggles, and above all, your courage to face your own learned silence, never ceased to amaze me. It was such a privilege to work with each of you and I thank you for choosing me to witness your journey. I wish you all the very best of everything as you speak and speak and speak.

Elizabeth Downing, thank you for designing my websites. You are an artist who somehow knows what I am imagining and then creates a website that is more wonderful than I could've imagined.

Julia Mitchell, thank you for your PR skills and keeping an eye out for what may be a good opportunity or contact for me.

And last but definitely not least, I want to thank the women in my family, my grandmother, mother, mother-in-law and sister for teaching me about your own experiences of silence. Your lessons have shaped my life for the better.

For information about Rosjke's work
visit: **www.thesilentfemalescream.com**

For information about Women's Power Circles
visit: **www.womenspowercircles.com**

- Sign up for Rosjke's free E-Newsletter

- Mother-Daughter Workshops

- Join a Women's Circle

- Articles on the Mother-Daughter Relationship

- Counselling for Women

Printed in July 2023
by Rotomail Italia S.p.A., Vignate (MI) - Italy